Earth
Sciences

PRENTICE HALL GENERAL REFERENCE
15 Columbus Circle
New York, New York 10023

Library of Congress Cataloging in Publication Data

Illustrated dictionary of earth sciences.
    The Prentice Hall illustrated dictionary of earth sciences /
    contributors, Martin Walters, Felicity Trotman.
        p.   cm.
    Previously published as: The illustrated dictionary of earth
    sciences. 1991.
        Summary: Presents an illustrated dictionary of earth science terms.
    ISBN 0–13–681735–1
        1. Earth sciences – Dictionaries. Juvenile. [1. Earth sciences –
    Dictionaries.] I. Walters, Martin. II. Trotman, Felicity. III. Title.
    QE5.134 1992
    550′.3–dc20
                                                            92–15822

10 9 8 7 6 5 4 3 2 1

Manufactured in Great Britain by BPCC Hazells Ltd.

Originally published in Great Britain by Merlion Publishing Ltd. as
THE ILLUSTRATED DICTIONARY OF EARTH SCIENCES in a
different form.

A Prentice Hall Illustrated Dictionary

Earth Sciences

Contributors
Martin Walters
Felicity Trotman

PRENTICE HALL GENERAL REFERENCE

New York · London · Toronto · Sydney · Tokyo · Singapore

Reader's notes

The entries in this dictionary have several features to help you broaden your understanding of the word you are looking up.

- Each entry is introduced by its headword. All the headwords in the dictionary are arranged in alphabetical order.

- Each headword is followed by a part of speech to show whether the word is used as a noun, adjective, verb, or prefix.

- Each entry begins with a sentence that uses the headword as its subject.

- Words that are bold in an entry are cross references. You can look them up in this dictionary to find out more information about the topic.

- The sentence in italics at the end of an entry helps you to see how the headword can be used.

- Many of the entries are accompanied by illustrations. The labels on the illustrations highlight the key points of information and will help you to understand some of the science behind the entries.

- Many of the labels on the illustrations have their own entries in the dictionary and can therefore be used as cross references.

abrasion   *noun*
Abrasion is the process of rubbing or wearing away. Sand blown across a rock face by wind can cause abrasion.
The surface of the rocks had been worn down by abrasion.

abrasive   *noun*
An abrasive is a rough substance used for rubbing down or polishing something. **Emery** is an example of an abrasive found in nature.
Sand blown by wind acts as an abrasive against rock.
abrasive   *adjective*

abyss   *noun*
An abyss is a deep cave or valley. A deep valley on the ocean floor is also often called an abyss.
The divers descended into the narrow abyss at the bottom of the sea.

abyssal plain   *noun*
The abyssal plain is the name given to the deepest part of the ocean floor. It is almost level and lies at a depth of between about 13,000 feet and 20,000 feet.
No light ever reaches the abyssal plain.

acid   *noun*
An acid is a kind of harsh **chemical** containing hydrogen that dissolves in water to make an acidic solution. Many acids can dissolve metals. An acid is the opposite of an **alkali**.
Strong acids are dangerous and can sting or burn the skin.
acidic   adjective

acid rain   *noun*
Acid rain is rain that is polluted by weak nitric and sulfuric acid. The acids are made when sulfur dioxide and nitric oxide, released into the air by burning **fossil fuels**, combine with water **vapor**.
Acid rain kills trees and fish and eats away rocks.

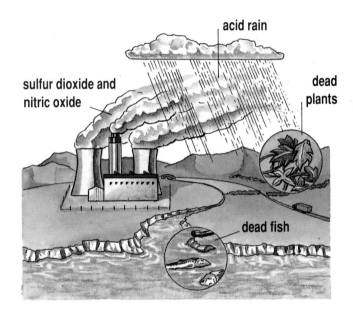

acid soil   *noun*
Acid soil contains minerals rich in hydrogen and aluminum which most plants need to grow. Water can **leach** minerals, such as calcium, magnesium, potassium, and sodium, out of the soil.
Some mosses grow well in acid soil.

acid water   *noun*
Acid water is water that contains weak carbonic **acid**. The water reacts with carbon dioxide in the **atmosphere** and in plants to make the acid. Carbonic acid reacts with many **minerals**.
The acid water turned the iron to rust.

active   *adjective*
Active is a word that describes **volcanoes** that **erupt** from time to time. Volcanoes that have not erupted for a long period are called **dormant**.
Smoke poured out of the active volcano.

aeolian *adjective*
Aeolian is a word that describes the action of the **wind**. Aeolian **erosion** occurs when the wind carries sand or other hard particles and these wear away soil and rocks.
The scientists could see that the aeolian erosion was wearing away the surface of the rock.

aerial *adjective*
Aerial describes an object that is airborne. Birds and other animals that feed on flying insects are known as aerial predators.
The shooting stars made a marvelous aerial display.

aftershock *noun*
Aftershock is the name given to shocks, or **tremors**, that follow an **earthquake**. The aftershock occurs minutes, hours, or even months after the first shock of an earthquake has faded away.
The aftershock caused even more damage than the earthquake itself.

agate *noun*
The mineral agate is a form of **quartz**. Agate usually has a banded pattern on its surface. Polished agate is used in jewelery as a semiprecious stone.
Onyx is a black-and-white form of agate.

agate · banded pattern

aggregate *noun*
An aggregate is a type of soil made up of tiny rock particles that stick together. Aggregate also describes the sand and gravel that is mixed with **cement** to make concrete.
The sidewalk was paved with a mixture of aggregate and cement.

agriculture *noun*
Agriculture is the practice of growing crops and raising livestock for food.
Flat, fertile soils are the best for agriculture.

air *noun*
Air is the mixture of **gases** that surrounds the Earth. Air is mostly made up of **nitrogen** and **oxygen**. It also contains **carbon dioxide**, **argon**, and water **vapor**.
The air was so clear that we could see the hills in the distance.

air pressure ► atmospheric pressure

alabaster *noun*
A mineral, alabaster is a form of **gypsum**. Alabaster is a soft rock and can be carved easily. Alabaster can also be polished to give it a smooth, shiny surface.
She carved a model of a bird out of alabaster.

alkali *noun*
An alkali is a kind of chemical **compound** that can neutralize **acids**. An alkali is the opposite of an acid.
Some strong alkalis are used in industry to clean machinery.
alkaline *adjective*

alloy *noun*
An alloy is a kind of solid substance made by melting a **metal** and mixing in smaller amounts of other metals or non-metals. The mixture is then cooled until it becomes solid.
Brass is an alloy that is made from copper and zinc.

alluvial fan   *noun*
An alluvial fan is a fan-shaped spread of **gravel**, **sand**, or **soil** deposited by mountain streams or **rivers**. When a stream leaves the hills, it flows more slowly across a valley or plain to form an alluvial fan. Alluvial fans are common in dry regions.
The soil of an alluvial fan may be very fertile.

alluvium   *noun*
Alluvium is a **deposit** of **sand**, **mud**, or **gravel**. Alluvium is left by a **river** when it leaves hilly ground and flows more slowly over flatter land.
The soil of the valley was a rich alluvium.

alpine   *adjective*
Alpine describes land that lies above the **tree line** on **mountains**. The name comes from the Alps of Europe, but is used for all such areas in the world. Alpine areas are very rocky, the soil is usually shallow, and the climate is cold.
There was not enough soil in the alpine region for a tree to grow roots.

altimeter   *noun*
An altimeter is an instrument for measuring height, or **altitude**. Some simple altimeters work by measuring **atmospheric pressure**, which grows weaker as the distance of the air from Earth increases. Aircraft altimeters measure the time it takes a radio signal to travel from the aircraft to the ground and back again.
The pilot could judge the plane's altitude by reading the altimeter.

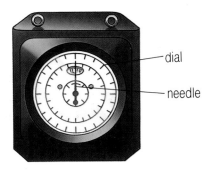

dial

needle

altitude   *noun*
Altitude describes the vertical distance, or height, of one point above another point. The altitude of land is usually measured from **sea level**.
Aircraft and migrating birds sometimes fly at a very high altitude above the Earth's surface.

altocumulus   *adjective*
Altocumulus describes a kind of **cloud** that is white, fluffy, and rounded and appears during fine weather.
Altocumulus clouds dotted the blue sky on the warm day.

altostratus   *adjective*
Altostratus describes a kind of **cloud** that is dark gray and forms a continuous sheet across the sky.
The altostratus clouds blotted out the Sun.

aluminum   *noun*
The **element** aluminum is a bright, silvery **metal**. Aluminum is extracted from an ore called **bauxite**, which is a kind of aluminum oxide. It resists corrosion.
Aluminum is useful for making machinery and aircraft bodies because it is light and strong.

amber   *noun*
Amber is a clear orange or cloudy yellow **mineral** that can be used as a **gem**. Amber comes from the liquid sap, or resin, which oozed from trees many millions of years ago. Some pieces of amber have insects trapped in them. Amber is found in **sedimentary** rocks and washed up on **seashores**.
She wore a necklace made from yellow amber.

amethyst *noun*
Amethyst is a **mineral**. A precious stone that is purple in color, amethyst is a kind of **quartz**.
The brooch had a large amethyst in the center.

ammonite *noun*
Now extinct, an ammonite was a kind of shellfish called a mollusk. Ammonites had hard, chalky, spiral shells. The shells can be found as **fossils** in some kinds of **sedimentary** rock, which are important in dating **zones** of **Mesozoic** rocks.
The fossil collection contained several large ammonites.

anemometer *noun*
An anemometer is an instrument that measures the speed of the **wind**. In the most common type of anemometer, the wind turns small cups that are attached to a rod. The harder the wind is blowing, the faster the cups turn.
The anemometer showed that the wind was at storm force.

aneroid barometer *noun*
An aneroid barometer measures **atmospheric pressure**. An aneroid barometer contains a metal box with a **vacuum** inside. The box has flexible sides that change shape as the weight of the air above changes.
Aneroid barometers have mostly replaced the older mercury barometers.

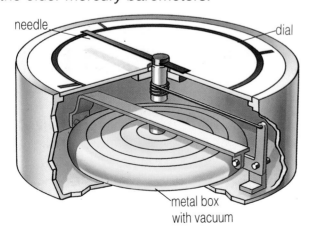

needle — dial — metal box with vacuum

Antarctic Circle *noun*
The Antarctic Circle is an imaginary line around the Earth, surrounding **Antarctica**. The position of the Antarctic Circle is at 66 degrees 30 minutes south of the Equator.
The Antarctic Circle lies about 1,200 miles south of New Zealand.

Antarctica *noun*
Antarctica is the Earth's most southerly **continent**, surrounding the South Pole. Most of the land is covered by **ice**. Antarctica is the coldest continent on Earth.
The scientists went to Antarctica to study different kinds of ice.

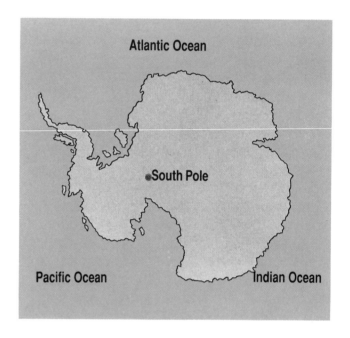

Atlantic Ocean
South Pole
Pacific Ocean
Indian Ocean

anthracite *noun*
Anthracite is a kind of **coal**. It is hard, black, and shiny and is the purest form of coal. Anthracite is more than 90 percent **carbon** and makes very little smoke when it burns.
Anthracite is preferred to other kinds of coal for a fuel because it is nearly smokeless.

anti- *prefix*
Anti- is a prefix meaning against or preventing.
He added antifreeze to the water to lower its freezing point.

anticline *noun*
An anticline is a fold in the **strata** of **rocks**. The fold has the shape of an arch, with the youngest **layers** of rocks at the top. Anticlines are caused by pressure on the rocks from the sides. The opposite of an anticline is a **syncline**.
Anticlines provide scientists with an opportunity to study stresses on the Earth's surface.

rock strata
young rock
old rock

anticyclone *noun*
An anticyclone is an area of high **atmospheric pressure**. Anticyclones almost always bring clear skies and settled **weather**. The opposite of an anticyclone is a **depression**, which is sometimes known as a **cyclone**.
The anticyclone signaled the hot, dry weather to come.

aquamarine *noun*
The **mineral** aquamarine is a precious stone that is green or turquoise in color. Aquamarine is a form of **beryl**.
He wore a ring that was set with aquamarines.

aqueous *adjective*
Aqueous describes substances that are liquid or that contain water.
The powder was dissolved in an aqueous solution.

Archean *adjective*
Archean is the name given to the second earliest **eon** in **geological time**. Some scientists believe the Archean Eon lasted from about 4,000 million years ago to about 2,500 million years ago. It is part of **Precambrian** era.
Many of the oldest rocks were formed during the Archean Eon.

archipelago *noun*
An archipelago is a group of **islands**. The islands in an archipelago are usually small, and they often form a line or a curved pattern.
The Society Islands form an archipelago in the south Pacific Ocean.

Arctic *noun*
The Arctic is the name given to the most northerly region of the world. It lies within the **Arctic Circle**. Northern Canada, much of Greenland, and the northern Soviet Union all lie within the Arctic region.
In some parts of the Arctic, the seas are always frozen.

North Pole
Arctic Ocean
Greenland
Canada

Arctic Circle *noun*
The Arctic Circle is an imaginary line around the Earth, to the north of which lies the **Arctic** region. The position of the Arctic Circle is at 66 degrees 17 minutes north of the **Equator**.
Iceland lies just below the Arctic Circle.

argon *noun*
The **element** argon is a **gas** that is found in the Earth's atmosphere. It makes up about 1 percent of the air. Argon is an **inert** gas so it does not react with other chemicals and does not form **compounds**.
Some kinds of light bulbs are filled with argon.

arid   *adjective*
Arid describes parts of the Earth that have a very dry **climate**, such as hot **deserts**. Arid regions get very little rain, or lose any water that falls as rain by **evaporation**. Most arid regions lie in the **tropics**.
The soil was so arid that no crops would grow.

arroyo   *noun*
An arroyo is a rocky **ravine**. Arroyos occur in dry areas and in **deserts**. They are a kind of dry river valley with steep sides and flat, sandy bottoms. Arroyos are found in the southwestern United States, in parts of India, and in South Africa.
The travelers found the heat of the arroyo too strong for hiking.

artesian well   *noun*
An artesian well is a well that provides **water** without a pumping mechanism. The well draws up water that has been held under pressure between layers of **impermeable** rock.
The artesian well gave a continuous supply of water to the valley.

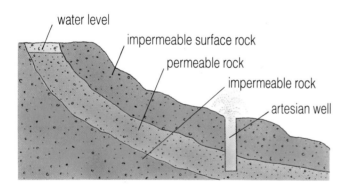

asbestos   *noun*
Asbestos is a **mineral** with a rough, thread-like texture. It is a **silicate**. Asbestos does not burn and can be used to protect objects from damage by flames. Asbestos is also resistant to most chemicals. However, breathing asbestos dust is harmful.
Asbestos can be woven into a cloth which resists heat.

asphalt   *noun*
Asphalt is a thick, sticky substance. Asphalt forms when petroleum is distilled or when it evaporates.
Asphalt is mixed with stones or chips for making roads or for covering roofs.

atlas   *noun*
An atlas is a collection of **maps**. Some atlases include maps of the whole world, others may show details of just one or a few countries. Maps of the stars and planets can also be found in atlases.
They found a map of the Arctic region in the world atlas.

atmosphere   *noun*
The atmosphere is the layer of **gases** around the **Earth**. The atmosphere can be divided into a number of smaller layers. The **troposphere** is nearest to the ground and contains the **air** we breathe.
The Earth's atmosphere acts like a blanket, trapping warmth near the surface.

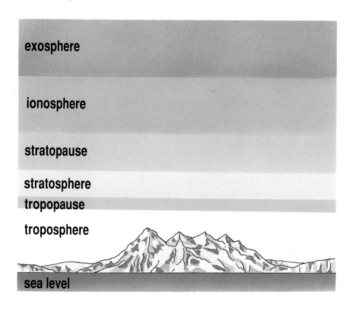

atmospheric pressure   *noun*
Atmospheric pressure measures the weight of the **air** that presses down on the surface of the Earth. Atmospheric pressure is measured in **bars**.
Atmospheric pressure is highest at ground level or sea level and gets lower with altitude.

basin *noun*
A basin is a **hollow** in the landscape. It has smooth sides and is shaped like a bowl. A basin is also the area of land drained by a **river** and its **tributaries**.
We could see hills rising at the sides of the basin.

bathyscaphe *noun*
A bathyscaphe is a kind of small, **submersible vehicle** used to explore deep water. A bathyscaphe usually has room for just one or two people who can look out at the sea through the windows in safety. It can move about freely under the water.
The bathyscaphe took them slowly down toward the seabed.

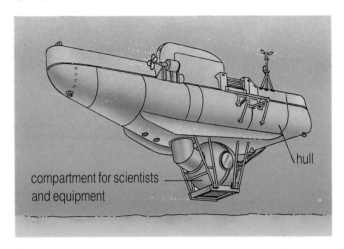

compartment for scientists and equipment — hull

bauxite *noun*
Bauxite is a **mineral** that contains the metal **aluminum**, found mostly in the warmer parts of the world. Almost all aluminum is obtained from bauxite.
The earth had been removed from one side of the hill to mine the bauxite underneath.

bay *noun*
A bay is an area of the sea that is enclosed by a curved section of **coast**. Bays vary in size from several hundred feet to thousands of miles across. The Bay of Bengal is the name of the huge bay in the Indian Ocean that lies between India and Burma.
He saw the lighthouse shining across the water from the other side of the bay.

beach *noun*
A beach is the strip of sloping land which lies along the **sea shore** between the high and low water level of the **tides**. Beaches are usually made of sand, gravel, or pebbles. A beach is formed by the action of waves grinding down small pieces of material from the rocks or soil at the land's edge.
The beach at the base of the cliff sloped down into the sea.

beacon *noun*
A beacon is a bright light or other strong signal that can be easily seen. Beacons are used to guide ships and airplanes on a safe course.
The lighthouse acted as a beacon to warn the fishing boat that it was near rocks.

bearing *noun*
A bearing is a way of measuring direction. Ships at sea work out their direction in bearings, measured in degrees using a **compass**.
The climber used a compass to find his bearings in the mountains.

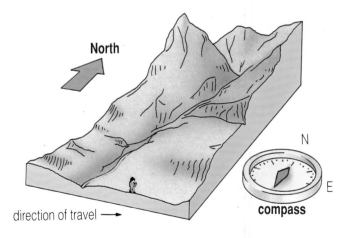

North

direction of travel →

N

E

compass

Beaufort Scale ► page 14

bed *noun*
A bed is a word used in **geology** to describe a **layer**, or **stratum**, of **sedimentary** rock.
The fossils were found close together in the same bed of rock.

13

Beaufort Scale *noun*

The Beaufort Scale is a scale that is used to measure the force of the **wind**. The scale goes from calm, force 0, to **hurricane**, force 12.

A storm is force 10 on the Beaufort Scale.

1 light air

2 light breeze
smoke drifts gently

3 gentle breeze
wind vane moves

4 moderate breeze
leaves and twigs in constant motion

5 fresh breeze
wind raises dust and leaves
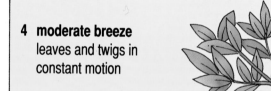

6 strong breeze
small trees and leaves sway

7 near gale
whole trees in motion

8 gale
twigs break from trees

9 strong gale
slight damage to buildings

10 storm
trees uprooted

11 violent storm
widespread damage

12 hurricane
widespread damage to buildings
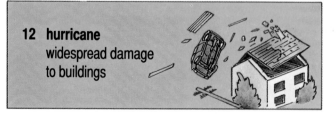

bedrock　*noun*
Bedrock is the solid rock beneath the surface of the Earth. In most places, the bedrock is covered by layers of loose rock or soil.
After digging down through the soil, we came to the hard bedrock.

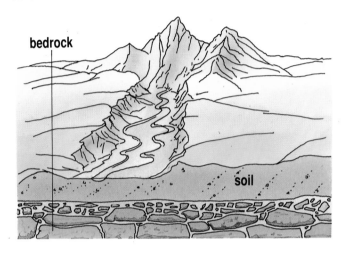

benthic　*adjective*
Benthic describes the area at the bottom of the sea. It also describes the animals and plants living there. On the **continental shelf** and near the **sea shore**, the benthic zone is very shallow. In the deep sea, the benthic zone is about 3,300 feet deep. The opposite of benthic is **pelagic**.
A trawl net is used to collect benthic fish from the sea bed.

benthos　*noun*
Benthos is the name used for the plants and animals living on the seabed, or in the **benthic** zone. The benthos includes seaweeds, and sea creatures such as crabs, shellfish, and flatfish.
The benthos of the continental shelf includes a great variety of animals.

beryl　*noun*
Beryl is a **mineral** found mostly in **granite** rocks. Beryl contains the elements **beryllium**, **aluminum**, **silicon**, and **oxygen**. The metal beryllium is made from beryl **crystals**.
The precious stones emerald and aquamarine are forms of beryl.

beryllium　*noun*
The **element** beryllium is found in the mineral **beryl**. It is a metal similar to **aluminum** and is used for making **alloys**.
Beryllium is made from ore containing beryl crystals.

bight　*noun*
A bight is a very large **bay** surrounded by the lands of a **continent**.
The Bight of Benin lies off the west coast of Africa.

bio-　*prefix*
Bio- is a prefix that is used to refer to living things.
The biochemist studied the chemistry of plants and animals.

biogas　*noun*
Biogas is a gas given off when waste materials **decompose**. The main gas produced in this way is **methane**, which can be collected and burned to provide heat **energy**.
Manure and food waste are good sources of biogas.

biological　*adjective*
Biological is used to describe living organisms. For example, biological science is the study of living things.
The region's unusual animals and plants proved to be of great biological interest.

biomass　*noun*
Biomass is a word that describes the total amount of living things in a particular area.
An area of tropical rain forest has a large biomass.

biosphere　*noun*
The biosphere is the name given to the parts of the Earth where living things are found. The biosphere is also called the **global** ecosystem.
The atmosphere, the seas, and the surface of the Earth all make up the biosphere.

bismuth *noun*
The **element** bismuth is a **metal**. **Alloys** of bismuth melt at low temperatures. Because they melt first, they are used as a safety device in many machines. Before the machines get too hot, the alloys melt and the machines stop working. Bismuth is also used to make some medicines.
There are large deposits of bismuth in Bolivia.

bitumen *noun*
Bitumen is an oily **compound** formed by the **evaporation** of petroleum. Solid forms of bitumen are also called **asphalt**.
The intense heat of the midday Sun left pools of bitumen on the road.

blizzard *noun*
A blizzard is a fierce **storm** of **snow**. Blizzards are common in open, icy regions such as the **Arctic** and **Antarctica**.
During a blizzard, snow is often blown into deep drifts.

block mountain *noun*
A block mountain is a **mountain** formed when two parts of the Earth's **crust** collide with each other, trapping a third part. The trapped section is pushed up between the other parts to form a mountain. Block mountains are often flat at the top, like Table Mountain in South Africa.
The block mountain towered over the surrounding land.

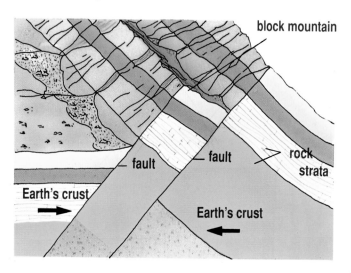

blowhole *noun*
A blowhole is a hole or **cave** in a sea **cliff**. Blowholes are found in areas where some of the rock in the cliffs has been **eroded** more than others. Large waves trap air in the caves, which then escapes as a spray through the blowhole when the **tide** is high.
As the waves entered the cave, sea water spouted out through the blowhole.

bluff *noun*
A bluff is a steep **cliff**. Bluffs may be found at the edge of a **valley**, or at the **sea shore**.
The climber stopped at the top of the bluff to take a good look at the valley below.

bog *noun*
A bog is an area of marshy ground where the soil is made up of wet **peat**. Bogs are made of thousands of moss plants that grow in water and are known as bog mosses. When the older moss plants die, their remains gradually **decompose**. In most bogs, a new layer of plants will grow on top of the dead material.
The soil in the bog was very acidic.

borax *noun*
The **mineral** borax contains **boron**, **sodium**, **hydrogen**, and **oxygen**. Borax is used for softening water and for cleaning.
Borax is used to make a special kind of glass that does not melt or crack when heated.

16

bore *noun*
A bore is a kind of **wave** that moves steadily up a **river**, traveling against the usual flow of the water. Bores can be seen in funnel-shaped **estuaries** during very high **tides**.
In the Severn River in the British Isles, a famous bore can be seen when the tide flows toward the land.

bore *verb*
Bore is used to describe drilling through rocks. Special drills have to be used to bore through hard rocks.
The teams worked for many months to bore a tunnel through the cliffs.

boreal *adjective*
Boreal describes the **region** of the Earth that lies south of the **Arctic**. In the boreal region, the main type of vegetation is the boreal forest, or **taiga**, made up mostly of cone-bearing or coniferous trees.
The boreal forests of Siberia stretch for thousands of miles.

boron *noun*
Boron is a rare **element** only found in **compounds** with other substances. Boron is usually found as boric acid or as **borax**.
Boron is extracted from rocks containing borax.

boulder *noun*
A boulder is a large **rock** that usually has rounded sides. Boulders are often found on mountain sides, at the foot of **cliffs** or on **scree** slopes.
We sheltered from the wind behind a boulder.

breach *noun*
A breach is a crack or hole in a hard surface. During a violent storm, **breakers** may make a breach in a seawall. The action of **weathering** may also cause a breach in a rock face.
The breach in the river bank caused the fields to be flooded.

breaker *noun*
Breakers are very large and powerful **waves** that occur on **coasts** facing the open **ocean**. Breaker waves are common near **reefs** and around rocky islands.
Surfers find the huge breakers off the coast of California especially challenging.

breccia *noun*
Breccia is a kind of **sedimentary** rock with a very coarse texture. It is made up of many sharp-sided pieces of rock of different sizes. All these pieces of rock are cemented together.
The rocks at the sides of the valley contained large amounts of breccia.

breeze *noun*
A breeze is a **wind** of medium strength. A light breeze makes leaves rustle and blows at about 4 miles an hour. A strong breeze makes large branches sway and blows at about 22 miles an hour. Breezes measure between 2 and 6 on the **Beaufort Scale**.
The boat's sails began to fill out in the breeze.

brook *noun*
A brook is a small, clear **stream** which is often found in hilly areas.
The brook flowed swiftly over the stones in the mountains.

brown coal ► **lignite**

17

buoy *noun*
A buoy is a floating marker in the sea or in a river. Safe **channels** of deeper water are often shown by a line of buoys. Buoys also mark shallow water near the **coast**.
We steered the boat clear of the mud banks by following the buoys.

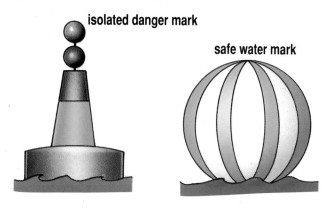
isolated danger mark
safe water mark

bush *noun*
Bush describes a habitat with many scattered trees and shrubs. Large areas of southern Africa and Australia are covered by bush.
The bush was so dry it caught fire easily.

butte *noun*
A butte is a flat-topped **hill** with steep rocky sides that is found in **arid** regions. A butte is formed when a **plateau** is **eroded** at the sides.
The butte stood out clearly from the plain below it.

rock strata

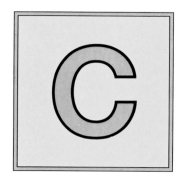

cadmium *noun*
The **element** cadmium is a bluish-white **metal**. Cadmium is often found in the same rocks as **copper** and **zinc**. Cadmium is used for making **alloys**, and **compounds** of cadmium are used in making television sets and batteries. Most cadmium comes from Japan.
Cadmium compounds are very poisonous.

calcite *noun*
Calcite is a white or colorless **mineral** made up of **crystals** of calcium carbonate. Most kinds of **limestone** are made of calcite.
Crystals of calcite can be seen without using a microscope.

calcium *noun*
The common **element** calcium is a **metal** that forms many **compounds** with other elements and is not found naturally in a pure form. **Limestone** is made of calcium, **carbon**, and **oxygen**. Plants and animals need calcium to grow properly.
Milk and cheese are good sources of calcium in the diet.

caldera *noun*
A caldera is a circular hole formed when a **volcano** erupts repeatedly. The eruptions dislodge the **cone** at the top of the volcano, leaving a large hole shaped like a **basin** at the center. A caldera can also be formed by the **erosion** of an **extinct** volcano. Sometimes, a lake fills the bottom of the caldera.
When we reached the edge of the caldera, we could see right down into the lake.

calm *adjective*
Calm describes gentle **weather** or sea conditions. In calm weather, there is little or no wind or rain. A calm sea has a flat surface or only very small waves. The opposite of calm is stormy.
They waited for calm weather to set sail.

Cambrian *adjective*
Cambrian describes a **period** in **geological time**. The Cambrian Period lasted from about 590 million years ago to about 505 million years ago. (See chart page 64.)
During the Cambrian Period, the climate was warm and wet.

canal *noun*
A canal is a straight waterway, built to carry ships or boats. Some canals link rivers together. Others connect two different **seas** or **oceans**. The Panama Canal, in Central America, allows ships to pass from the Atlantic Ocean to the Pacific Ocean and back. The Suez Canal links the Mediterranean Sea with the Red Sea.
The barges carried their cargo slowly along the canal.

canyon *noun*
A canyon is a deep **valley** with very steep sides. Canyons are usually found in flat, dry places and often have a river flowing through them. Some canyons are found on the **sea bed**.
The Grand Canyon, in the United States, is one of the natural wonders of the world.

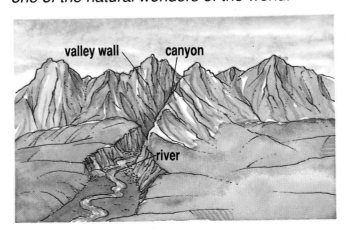

cape *noun*
A cape is a piece of **land** jutting into a **sea**. One of the most famous is the Cape of Good Hope, on the coast of South Africa.
The ship sailed around the cape.

carbon *noun*
Carbon is a nonmetallic **element**. Carbon is one of the most common elements. It is found in all living things, as well as in rocks, **coal**, **oil**, and other **minerals**. There are two forms of pure carbon: **graphite** and **diamond**.
All living things are made of compounds that contain carbon.

diamond   graphite

carbon dating *noun*
Carbon dating is a way of finding the age of an **organic** substance. Carbon dating measures the **radioactivity** of a type of carbon called carbon-14, which all organic substances contain.
The scientists determined the age of the fossil tree through carbon dating.

carbon dioxide *noun*
Carbon dioxide is a colorless, odorless **gas** found in small amounts in the air. The gas is formed when **compounds** containing **carbon** are burned and when animals and plants breathe.
Plants make their food using carbon dioxide.

carbon monoxide *noun*
Carbon monoxide is a colorless, odorless **gas** that is poisonous to breathe. Carbon monoxide is formed when **compounds** containing **carbon** are burned, but are not burned completely.
Exhaust from automobiles contains a mix of poisonous gases, including carbon monoxide.

19

carbonate   *noun*
A carbonate is a **salt** that is made from **carbon** and another **element**. **Chalk** and **limestone** are made up of calcium carbonate. Bones also contain sodium carbonate.
Scientists found the water to be rich in calcium carbonate.

Carboniferous   *adjective*
Carboniferous describes the **period** in **geological time** from about 360 million years ago to about 286 million years ago. (See chart page 64.)
Coal comes from the remains of trees and other plants that grew during the Carboniferous Period.

cardinal point   *noun*
A cardinal point is any one of the four main points of the **compass**. The cardinal points are north, south, west, and east.
The compass had the cardinal points clearly marked on its face.

carnelian   *noun*
Carnelian, or cornelian, is a semiprecious stone. A red or reddish-brown form of **chalcedony**, carnelian is found mostly in India, South America, and Japan. It has been used as a gem for thousands of years.
The ring had a carnelian at its center.

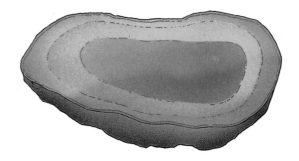

cartography   *noun*
Cartography is the process of making **maps**. A cartographer marks features of the land or sea on a map by symbols, **contour** lines, and shading.
The art of cartography has been aided by the use of satellite images of the Earth.

cascade   *noun*
A cascade is a series of **waterfalls** close together on a river. Cascades are usually found on fast-flowing mountain rivers.
The canoes had to be carried through the cascade.

cassiterite   *noun*
Cassiterite is a brown or black **mineral** containing **tin** and **oxygen**. Cassiterite is found mostly in **igneous** rocks.
Tin is extracted from cassiterite.

cat's eye   *noun*
Cat's eye is a precious stone, so-named because its pattern looks like a cat's eye. Cat's eye is a form of **quartz** found mainly in Sri Lanka.
Some of the precious stones were cat's eyes.

cataract   *noun*
A cataract is a kind of **waterfall** in which water flows very fast over a series of rocky falls. Cataracts are found in mountain areas where streams and rivers flow quickly.
We had to land the boat as we approached the cataract.

catchment area   *noun*
A catchment area is a piece of land drained by a **river** system. At the edge of one catchment area, the water drains in another direction into a different catchment area.
The rivers at either side of the valley flowed into the same catchment area.

cave ▶ page 22

Celsius *noun*
Celsius is the standard international **scale** that is used for measuring **temperature**. The Celsius scale is sometimes called the centigrade scale. In the United States, air temperatures are measured on the **Fahrenheit** scale.
Water freezes at 0 degrees Celsius and boils at 100 degrees Celsius.

cement *noun*
Cement is a substance that binds other materials together. In **sedimentary** rocks, cement is the material that binds pieces of rock together. Cement also describes a powdery mixture of **clay** and **lime**, which sets when water is added.
The cement set firmly and held the post upright.

Cenozoic *adjective*
Cenozoic describes the most recent **era** in **geological time**. The Cenozoic Era began about 65 million years ago and continues to the present day. It contains the **Quaternary** and **Tertiary** suberas. (See chart page 64.)
Few mammals lived before the Cenozoic Era.

centigrade ▶ **Celsius**

chalcedony *noun*
Chalcedony is a **mineral** found all over the world. It is a variety of **quartz** and is found in **volcanic** rocks. Many semiprecious **gems** are forms of chalcedony.
Agate, onyx, and bloodstone are all forms of chalcedony.

chalk *noun*
Chalk is a kind of **limestone** rock which is often pure white. It is made from the tiny shells of marine animals that died millions of years ago during the **Cretaceous** Period. Chalk is mostly calcium carbonate.
The White Cliffs of Dover in the British Isles are made of chalk.

channel *noun*
A channel is a groove in the Earth's surface cut by a river or a stream. The channel is cut out, or **eroded**, by the force of the flowing water. Near its source in high regions, a river flows down a rocky, narrow channel. In lowland areas, where the land slopes more gently, the channel fills up with **silt** and becomes wider.
During the floods, the river broke the banks of its usual channel.

chart *noun*
A chart is a kind of **map**. Weather forecasters use charts showing the **wind**, **temperature**, and **atmospheric pressure**. Sailors also use charts to map their position at sea.
The chart marked the rocks in the channel.

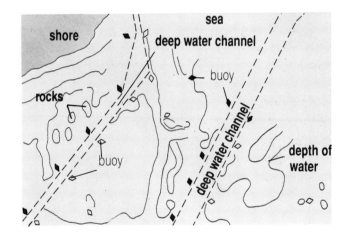

chemical *noun*
A chemical is any one of the individual, pure substances from which all materials are made. The simplest chemicals are the **elements**. Elements join together to make more complicated chemicals called **compounds**.
The sample of rock was tested to determine its chemical elements.

chert *noun*
Chert is a kind of **sedimentary** rock. It is often a dark color and is made up of tiny **crystals** of **quartz**. Chert usually forms on the sea-floor. **Flint** is one kind of chert.
Part of the cliff was made of gray chert.

21

cave   *noun*

A cave is a natural underground **hollow** found in **rock**, **earth**, or **ice**. Caves are usually made by the action of **water** wearing away the rock, soil, or ice. Very large caves are sometimes found in limestone rocks.
The waves had carved out a huge cave in the cliff.

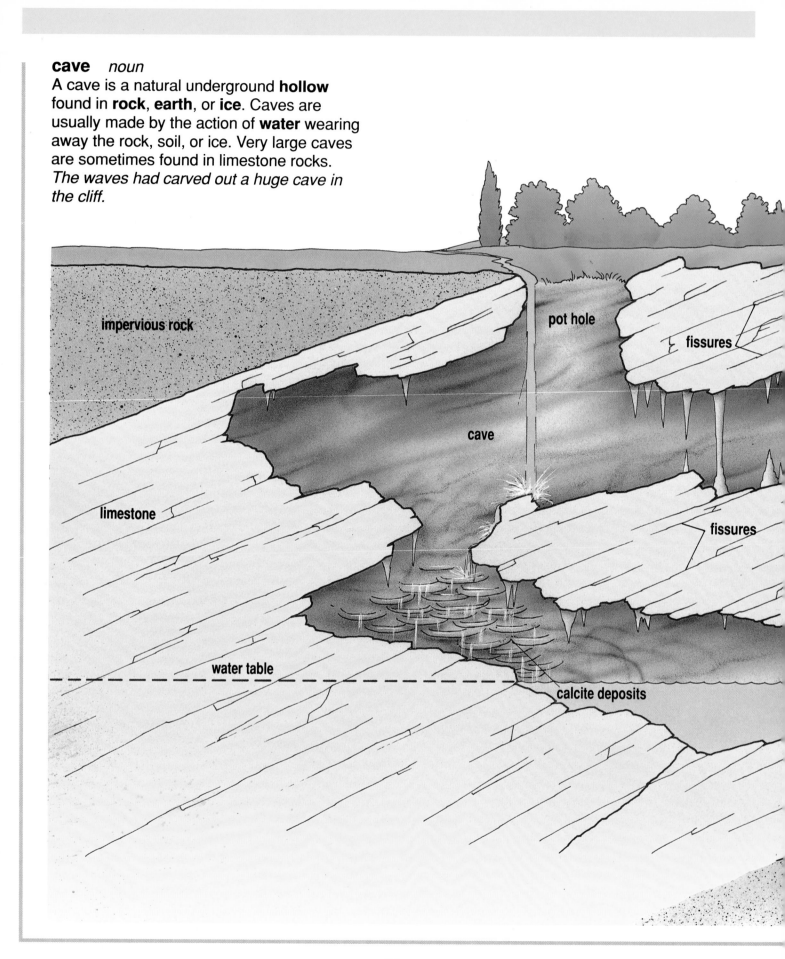

impervious rock

pot hole

fissures

cave

limestone

fissures

water table

calcite deposits

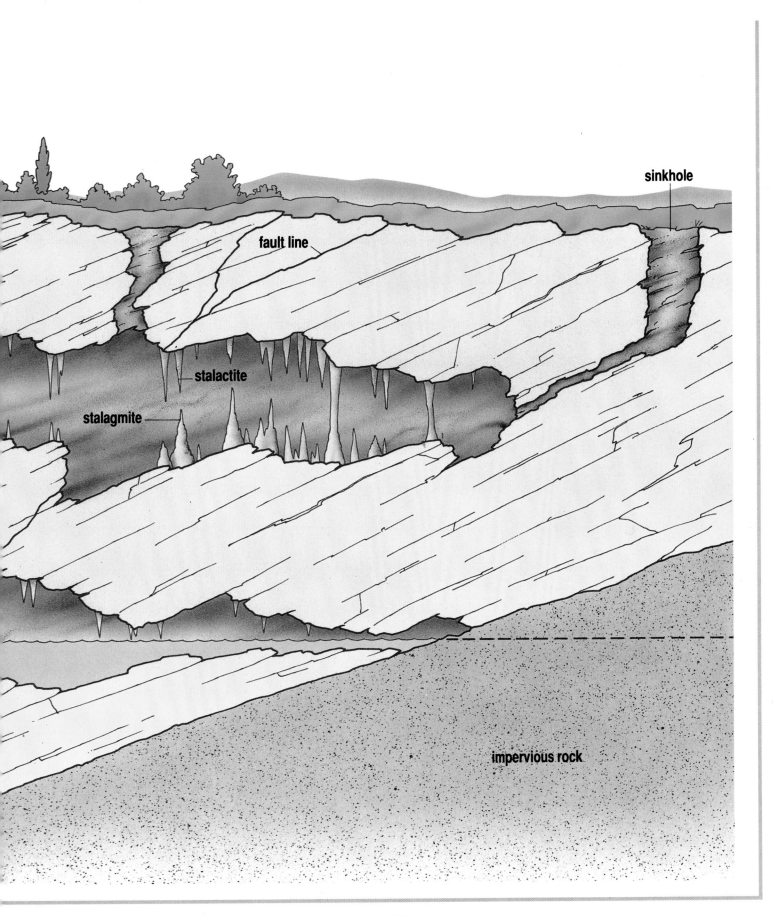

sinkhole

fault line

stalactite

stalagmite

impervious rock

China clay   *noun*
China clay, or **kaolin**, is a **mineral** containing **aluminum** and **silica**. China clay is used for making china and porcelain and also for making some kinds of paper.
The potter made a jug from China clay.

chinook   *noun*
The chinook is a kind of **wind**. The chinook is warm and dry and blows down the eastern side of the Rocky Mountains in the United States.
When the chinook blew, the snow melted very quickly.

chlorine   *noun*
The **element** chlorine is a greenish-yellow **gas**. In nature, it is only found in **compounds**, such as sodium chloride, which is the chemical name for common salt.
Chlorine is added to the water in swimming pools to kill germs.

chromium   *noun*
The **element** chromium is a hard, shiny **metal**. Chromium is used as a coating on steel to protect it from rust. Chromium is also used in **alloys**.
The bumper of the automobile was covered with a shiny coating of chromium.

cinnabar   *noun*
Cinnabar is a reddish **mineral** found mostly in **volcanic** rocks. Cinnabar is made of soft, red **crystals** and contains **mercury** and **sulfur**. It is occasionally used as a gemstone.
The factory extracted mercury from cinnabar.

circulation   *noun*
Circulation describes a cyclical movement in the air or water. The circulation of the water in the sea creates regular **currents**. The circulation of the air makes winds blow.
The circulation of water in the ocean kept the sea at a cool temperature near the coast.

cirrocumulus   *adjective*
Cirrocumulus describes a kind of **cloud** made of ice crystals found in the sky above a height of 3 miles. The clouds form long strips with rounded edges. (See illustration page 30.)
The sky was striped with cirrocumulus clouds.

cirrostratus   *adjective*
Cirrostratus describes a kind of **cloud** that forms high up and looks like a thin veil across the sky. These clouds form as a **warm front** approaches. (See page 30.)
The thin layer of cirrostratus clouds gradually covered the sky.

cirrus   *adjective*
Cirrus describes a kind of **cloud** that forms in the sky at a height of about 3 miles. The clouds have a wispy shape. (See illustration page 30.)
We saw thin bands of cirrus clouds streaked across the sky.

citrine *noun*
The **mineral** citrine is a yellow form of **quartz** very similar to **topaz**. It is found in parts of North America, South America, Russia, and the British Isles. Some citrines are cut and used as gemstones.
The rock contained pale yellow crystals of citrine.

clay *noun*
Clay is a mud-like substance formed from tiny pieces of rock. The **minerals** in clay are mostly made from **silicates**. Clay soaks up water easily and becomes sticky and soft. It cracks when dry.
The thick clay on the river bottom stuck to our feet.

cleavage *noun*
Cleavage describes the splitting of a rock or **mineral** to make flat surfaces. Some types of cleavage are very unusual and form only if a particular mineral is split.
The geologist tapped the mineral sharply with a hammer, to show the vertical cleavage.

cliff *noun*
A cliff is a steep rock face rising up from flat ground or the side of a mountain. Many rocky **islands** have high cliffs. Cliffs are very common at the **coast**, where waves have **eroded** the rocks.
The boat could not land because the island was surrounded by steep cliffs.

climate ► page 26

climatologist *noun*
A climatologist is a scientist who studies the **climates** around the world and observes how these climates differ from place to place.
Climatologists warn that the Earth's climate might change and cause flooding in some parts of the world.
climatalogy *noun*

cloud ► page 30

cloudburst *noun*
A cloudburst is a sudden, very heavy shower of rain. Cloudbursts usually happen in warm and stormy weather.
They were quickly soaked by the unexpected cloudburst.

coal *noun*
Coal is a kind of **deposit** that is rich in **carbon**. Coal forms when **organic** material, such as trees and other plants, is crushed for millions of years by layers of **sedimentary** rock. Coal is a **fossil fuel**.
Coal gives out heat when it is burned.

coast *noun*
The coast is the edge of the land where it meets the sea. Some coasts are gently sloping, with sandy **beaches**. Other coasts are wild and rocky.
The coast was constantly pounded by heavy waves.

cobalt *noun*
The **element** cobalt is a **metal**. It is used in making **magnets** and steel **alloys**, and a **compound** of cobalt is also used to make a bright blue color for paints.
The television set contained magnets made of cobalt.

climate *noun*

Climate describes the usual **weather** of a place or region. The climate can be affected by **temperature**, **rainfall**, **altitude**, and distance from the sea. **Polar**, **temperate**, **maritime**, **tropical**, **arid**, and

Mediterranean are some of the major types of climates in the world.

Countries close to the Equator have a tropical climate.

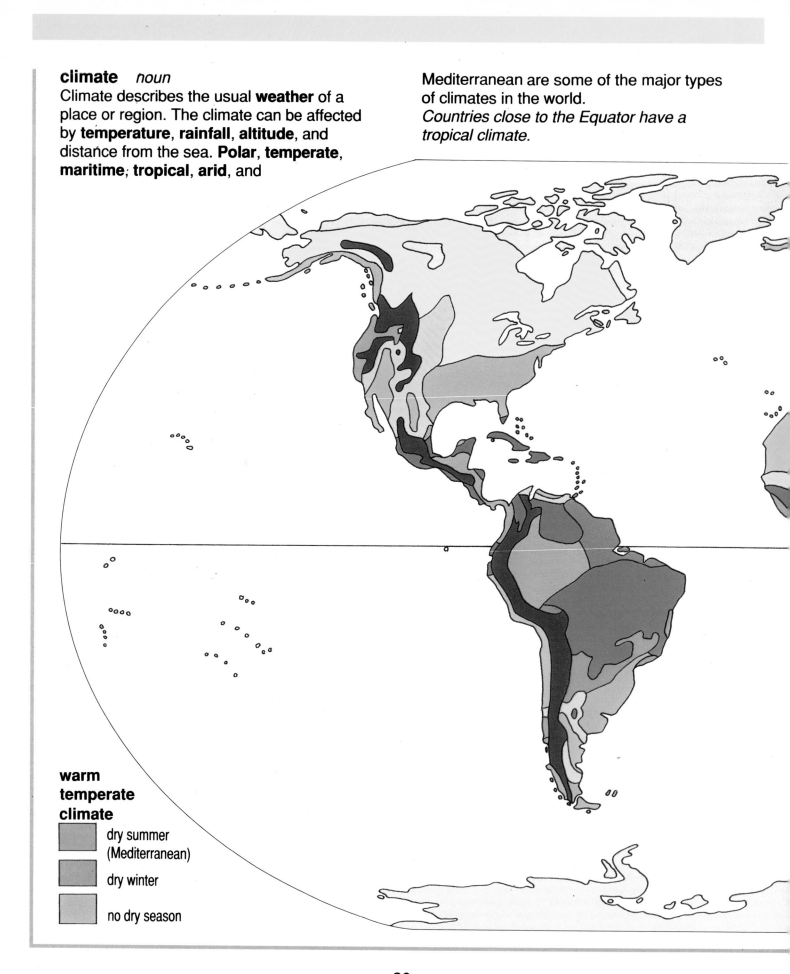

warm temperate climate

- dry summer (Mediterranean)
- dry winter
- no dry season

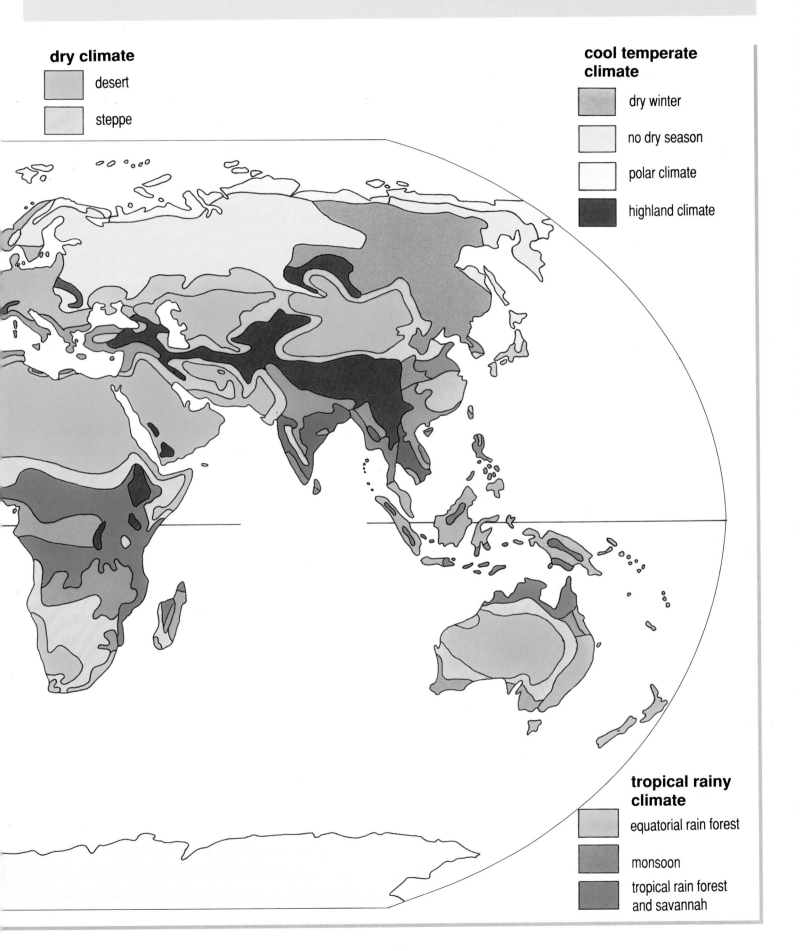

dry climate
- desert
- steppe

cool temperate climate
- dry winter
- no dry season
- polar climate
- highland climate

tropical rainy climate
- equatorial rain forest
- monsoon
- tropical rain forest and savannah

col *noun*
A col is a gap in a mountain or in a line of hills. It is often the point where roads and railways cross the mountains or hills because it is lower than the rest of the area. A col is also called a **pass** or saddle.
We walked through the col from one valley to the next.

cold front *noun*
A cold front is the meeting place between a mass of warm air and a mass of cold air. A cold front arrives when a **depression** passes, bringing colder air and higher pressure. **Cumulonimbus clouds** may form at a cold front.
The temperature fell very quickly as the cold front passed.

compass *noun*
A compass is used for working out a direction. Most compasses contain a needle which has been made into a **magnet** and always points to the Earth's **magnetic poles**.
We followed our trail using a map and a compass.

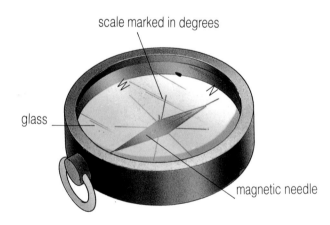

scale marked in degrees

glass

magnetic needle

composition *noun*
The composition of a substance is the total of all the **chemicals** it contains. The composition of the air is a mixture of gases, mainly nitrogen and oxygen.
The chemist analyzed the exact composition of the sample.

compound *noun*
A compound is a **chemical** substance that contains two or more **elements** joined together. Sodium chloride, or common salt, is a well-known chemical compound.
Chemists can split compounds into individual elements in the laboratory.

condensation *noun*
Condensation describes how a **gas** changes into a **liquid**. The most common kind of condensation is the change from water **vapor** to water. **Clouds** are formed by condensation of water vapor in the **atmosphere**. The word condensation is also used for the liquid itself.
The cold glass clouded over with condensation from the air.
condense *verb*

cone *noun*
A cone is a solid shape which is circular at the bottom and pointed at the top. A **volcano** is often described as cone-shaped. During an **eruption**, the top of the volcano's cone may be blown away.
The cone of the volcano towered over the landscape.

conglomerate *noun*
Conglomerate is a kind of **sedimentary** rock made up of small, rounded pebbles held together by a **cement**. The cement is usually made up of **calcites** or **silicates**.
Conglomerate often forms along river-beds or at beaches.

contaminate   *verb*
To contaminate is to make something less pure by adding another substance. Dangerous **chemicals** may contaminate drinking water. The ground near a nuclear reactor may be contaminated by **radioactivity**.
The air was contaminated by the dirty smoke from the factory.
contamination   *noun*

continent ▶ page 34

continental crust   *noun*
The continental crust is part of the outer shell of the Earth. The continental crust lies under the **continents** and has an average depth of about 20 miles. **Tectonic plates** are made up of continental crust and **oceanic crust**.
All the continents lie on the continental crust.

continental divide   *noun*
A continental divide is a chain of high mountains that separates one part of a **continent** from another.
The Rocky Mountains form a continental divide in North America.

continental drift   *noun*
Continental drift describes how **continents** move over the surface of the Earth. Some scientists think that all the continents have gradually moved apart from one large land mass, called **Pangaea**, by continental drift. Continental drift is part of the study of **plate tectonics**.
Some scientists believe that, millions of years in the future, continental drift will move Australia nearer to Asia.

continental shelf   *noun*
The continental shelf is the land that lies under the sea surrounding the **continents**. The width of the shelf varies from a couple of miles to about 250 miles. It slopes gently seaward. At the edge of the continental shelf, the sea bed drops away very steeply.
Countries bordering the Pacific Ocean often have a narrow continental shelf.

contour   *noun*
A contour is a line drawn on a **map**, or **chart**. Maps of the land have contours to show high and low ground. All the points joined by a contour line on a map are the same height above **sea level**. Maps of the sea have contours showing the depth of the water.
The contours showed that the hill was very steep.

view of hill from above

height in feet

side view of hill

300
200
100

sea level

300ft
200ft
100ft

contour lines

convection   *noun*
Convection describes the way in which a hot gas or liquid moves. If air or water is heated from below, it warms up. As this happens, the air or water takes up more space and starts to rise. As it rises, the air or water cools down. Because cool substance takes up less space, it then begins to fall.
The hot, sandy soil warmed the air above it and the air rose by convection.

convection current   *noun*
A convection current is the movement of a **gas** such as air caused by **convection**. During convection, the air or gas moves up or down. The movement is called a **current**.
Convection currents of air often develop above the ground on a sunny day.

29

cloud *noun*

A cloud is a collection of water **vapor** or ice crystals. Water drops form in clouds and fall as rain toward the ground. Some clouds form high in the **atmosphere**. Clouds which form close to the ground are called **mist** or **fog**. Types of clouds are illustrated below.

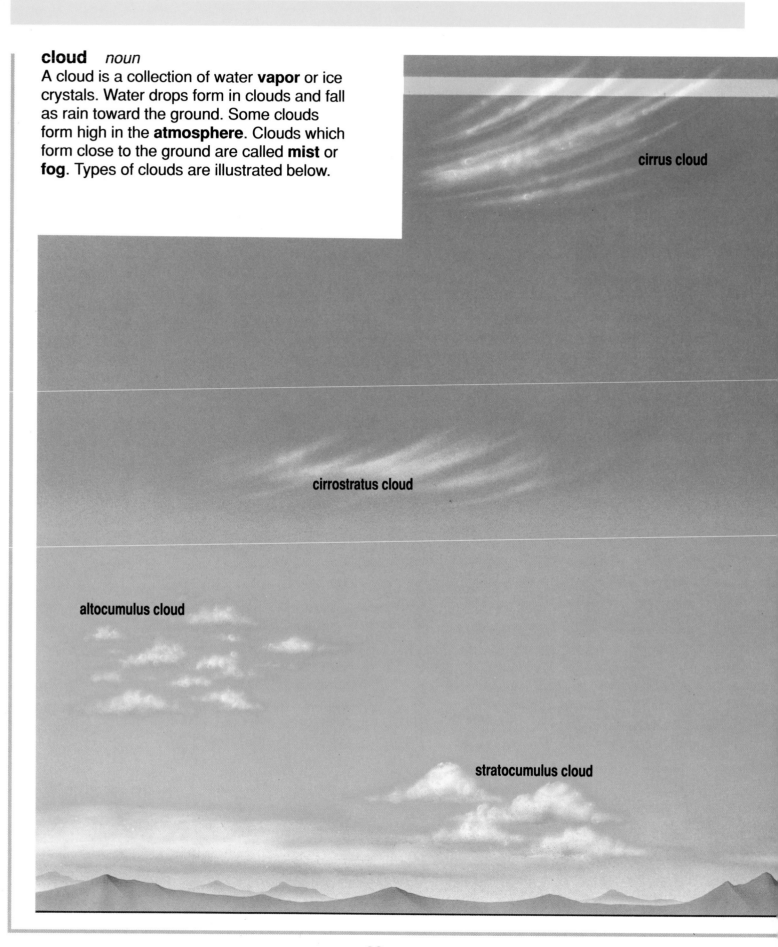

cirrus cloud

cirrostratus cloud

altocumulus cloud

stratocumulus cloud

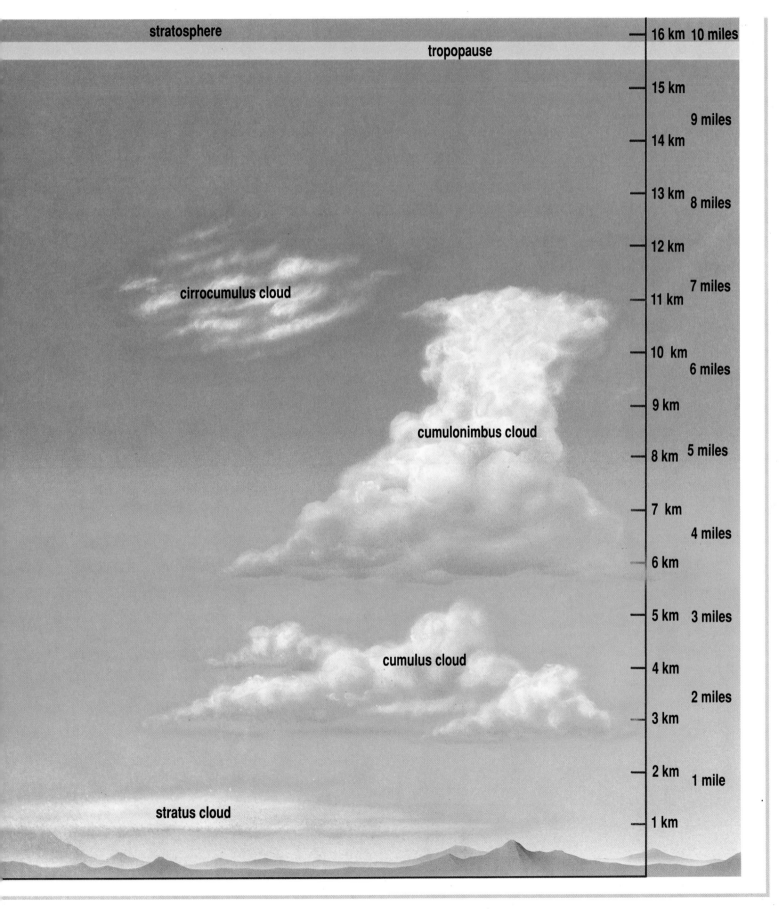

stratosphere

tropopause

cirrocumulus cloud

cumulonimbus cloud

cumulus cloud

stratus cloud

16 km 10 miles

15 km

9 miles

14 km

13 km 8 miles

12 km

7 miles

11 km

10 km 6 miles

9 km

8 km 5 miles

7 km

4 miles

6 km

5 km 3 miles

4 km

2 miles

3 km

2 km 1 mile

1 km

copper *noun*
The **element** copper is a soft, red-brown **metal**, electric wire and cooking pots are sometimes made from copper. The metal is also used to make **alloys**.
Copper wire is usually encased in plastic.

coral *noun*
A coral is a kind of **marine** animal with a hard skeleton. Corals belong to the same family as sea anemones. When the corals die, the skeletons build up to form a **coral reef**.
The warm sea contained millions of corals.

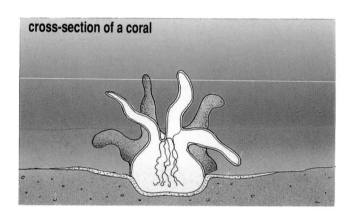
cross-section of a coral

coral island *noun*
A coral island is an island formed from a **coral reef**. Coral islands develop when the sea level drops and the reef shows above the surface of the water.
Many marine animals live on the coral island.

coral reef *noun*
A coral reef is a rock-like structure formed in clear, warm seas by colonies of tiny animals called **corals**. Their chalky skeletons build up over hundreds of years to make coral reefs.
The coral reef was dangerous to ships.

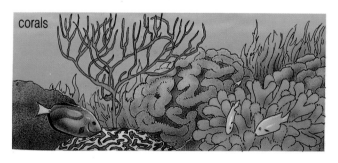
corals

cordillera *noun*
A cordillera is a group or chain of **mountains**, stretching across the land in a line. The Andes, in South America, are a famous cordillera.
The long line of the cordillera rose up in the distance.

core *noun*
The core is the innermost part of the **Earth**, lying about 1,750 miles below the surface of the Earth. The **inner core** is solid and is made mostly of **iron** and **nickel**. The **outer core** is liquid and is made mainly of molten rocks. The temperature of the core is about 2,700 degrees Celsius.
Scientists think the inner core of the Earth is very dense.

cornelian ► **carnelian**

corundum *noun*
Corundum is a very hard **mineral** made up of **aluminum** and **oxygen**. Red ruby and blue sapphire are forms of corundum. They are precious stones and are used to make jewellery. A very dark-coloured form of corundum is used in industry as an **abrasive**.
Ruby and sapphire are both forms of corundum.

cove *noun*
A cove is a small bay or inlet on the coast, which is sheltered by **headlands**. A cove is often rocky at the sides, but may have a sandy beach in the center.
The geologist discovered some unusual rocks on the beach of the cove.

crag *noun*
A crag is a steep rock jutting out from the side of a hill or a mountain. Some crags are made when **weathering** erodes the rock of a mountain.
The rock climbers used crags as visual landmarks when they explored the mountains.

crater *noun*
A crater is a hollow on the surface of a planet. Craters are circular in shape and have steep sides. They can be made by **meteorites** that crash into the planet. The mouth of a volcano is also called a crater.
Smoke rose threateningly from the crater of the volcano.

crater

volcano

creek *noun*
A creek is a narrow, winding **channel** with a stream at the bottom. Creeks are often found in muddy areas, such as **salt marshes**. Many creeks are flooded by the sea at high tide.
We jumped over the creek and walked across the marsh.

crest *noun*
A crest is the top of a hill or a mountain. From the crest of a hill, it is often possible to see down into the valleys on both sides.
We kept on walking upward until we reached the crest of the hill.

Cretaceous *adjective*
Cretaceous describes a **period** in **geological time** from about 144 million years ago to about 65 million years ago. (See chart page 64.)
The dinosaurs became extinct during the Cretaceous Period.

crevasse *noun*
A crevasse is a deep, steep-sided hole in the ice of an **ice field** or **glacier**. Crevasses are formed when the ice moves and splits. A crevasse can be hundreds of feet deep.
The explorers could not cross the crevasse safely.

crude oil *noun*
Crude oil is the heavy brown liquid petroleum that is first pumped out of the ground. Oil wells extract crude oil from **oil fields** deep under the ground or from under the sea. It is refined to make many petroleum products.
The earth around the well was stained brown with crude oil.

crust *noun*
The crust is the outermost part of the **Earth** made up mostly of **granite** and **basalt**. The **continental crust** is about 20 miles thick below the surface of the land. The **oceanic crust** is about 3 miles thick below the bottom of the sea.
The whole of the Earth's surface is covered by a crust.

crystal ► page 37

crystallize *verb*
Crystallize describes the way in which non living, or **inorganic**, matter grows into **crystals**. Gases, liquids, or solids may crystallize. Some substances crystallize as their water content evaporates. Other substances crystallize when they become very cold.
The water crystallized into ice in the freezing weather.

continent *noun*

A continent is a large **land-mass**. It is formed from **continental crust**, and rises steeply from the **ocean floor**. A continent contains a wide range of geological and geographical **features**. The seven continents are Asia, Africa, North America, South America, Antarctica, Europe, and Australia. Asia is the largest continent. The continent of North American stretches from the Atlantic Ocean to the Pacific Ocean.

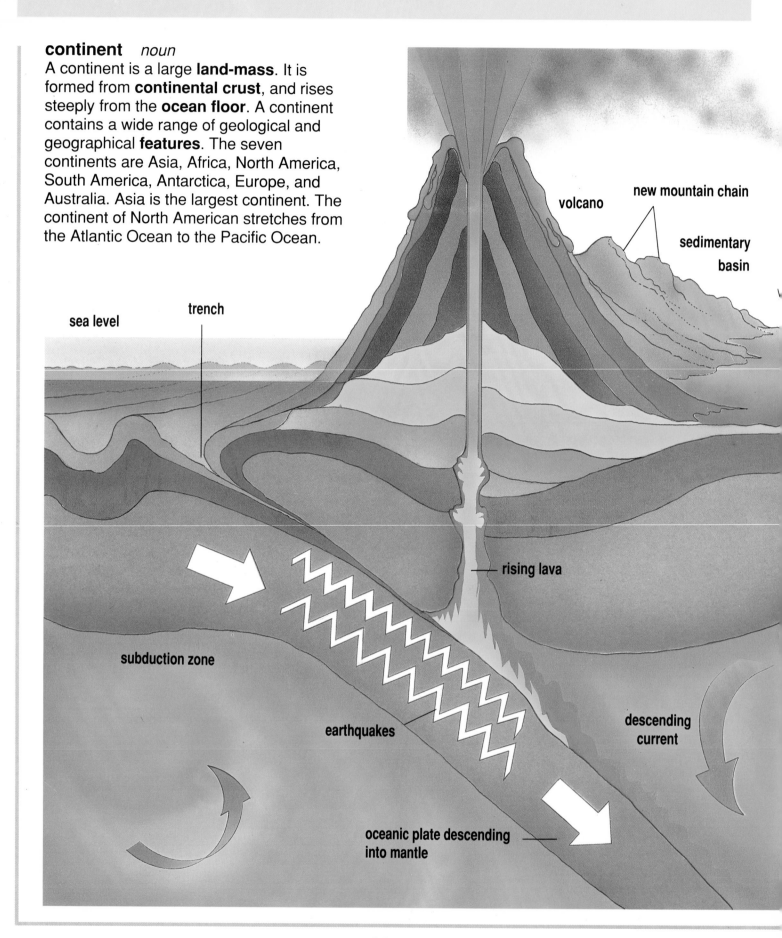

volcano

new mountain chain

sedimentary basin

sea level

trench

rising lava

subduction zone

earthquakes

descending current

oceanic plate descending into mantle

According to **plate tectonics**, the continents are always in motion and new features are formed as they collide along **subduction zones**.

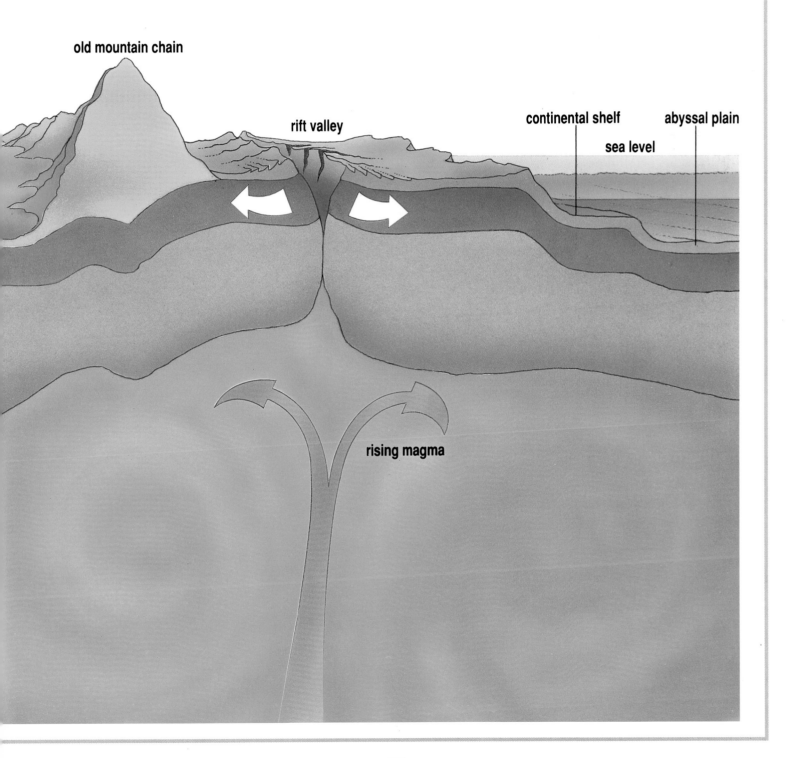

old mountain chain

rift valley

continental shelf

abyssal plain

sea level

rising magma

crystallography   *noun*
Crystallography is the study of the outer shape and inner structure of **crystals**.
Through crystallography, the characteristics of all the different minerals have been discovered.

cumulonimbus   *adjective*
Cumulonimbus **clouds** are very tall and gray and often spread out at the top. Cumulonimbus clouds bring heavy showers and storms. (See page 30.) **Tornadoes** sometimes come from these clouds.
Cumulonimbus clouds gathered before the storm.

cumulus   *adjective*
Cumulus **clouds** look rounded and fluffy and can be very tall. They are usually flat at the bottom. Cumulus clouds often develop in **convection currents** of warm air, particularly in hot weather. (See illustration page 30.)
The large cumulus clouds moved slowly across the sky.

current   *noun*
A current is a movement of air or water. In the sea, currents are caused by the rotation of the Earth and by the winds. In the **northern hemisphere**, the main ocean currents flow in a clockwise direction. In the **southern hemisphere**, they move in an anticlockwise direction. Air currents are caused by **convection**.
The Gulf Stream is the main current in the north Atlantic Ocean.

cycle   *noun*
A cycle is a process in which any material moves around in a system. Water moves in a cycle from the sea into the air by **evaporation**, and then falls as rain or snow onto the land. The water cycle is completed when the water gathers in rivers and flows to the sea.
Rainfall is an important part of the water cycle.

cyclone   *noun*
A cyclone is a very strong wind. Cyclones sometimes blow around an area of low **atmospheric pressure**, particularly in the **tropics**. A cyclone may also be called a **depression**.
The strong cyclone destroyed houses and brought flooding.

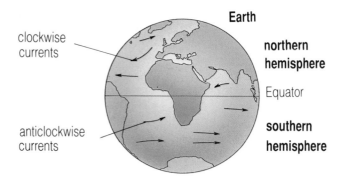

clockwise currents

Earth

northern hemisphere

Equator

anticlockwise currents

southern hemisphere

crystal   *noun*

A crystal is a solid with a regular shape, such as cubic or tetragonal. Crystals are often hard and shiny, and have smooth, flat surfaces. Most **minerals** are found naturally as crystals.

Grains of common salt and precious stones, such as diamonds, are crystals.

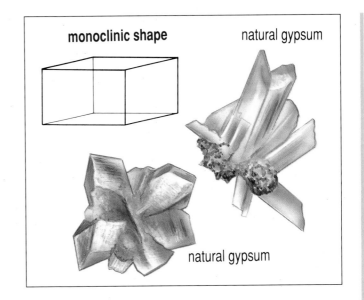

monoclinic shape

natural gypsum

natural gypsum

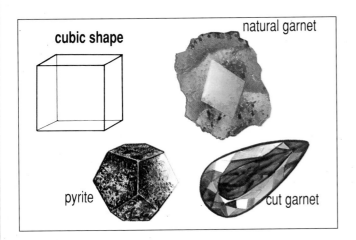

cubic shape

natural garnet

pyrite

cut garnet

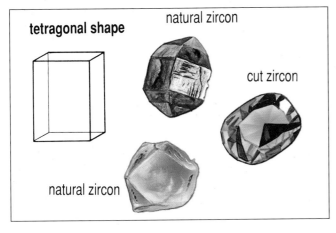

tetragonal shape

natural zircon

cut zircon

natural zircon

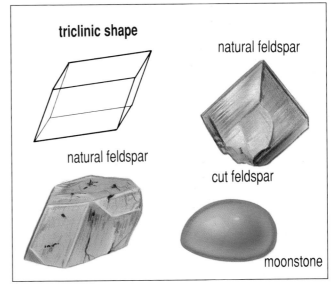

triclinic shape

natural feldspar

natural feldspar

cut feldspar

moonstone

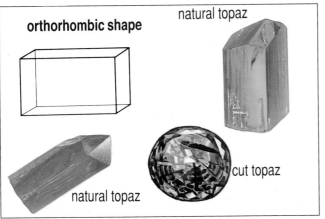

orthorhombic shape

natural topaz

cut topaz

natural topaz

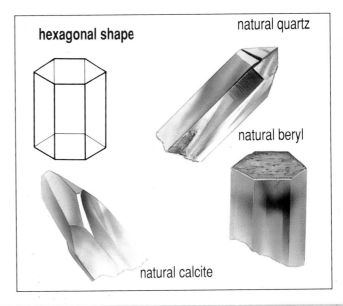

hexagonal shape

natural quartz

natural beryl

natural calcite

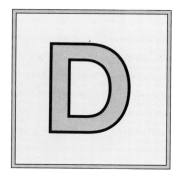

dam *noun*

A dam is a structure that controls the flow of water. Dams are built to hold water in **reservoirs**, or to stop flooding.
The valley flooded when the dam burst.

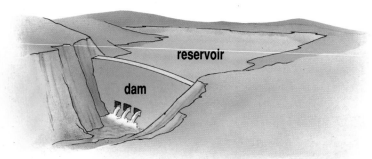

reservoir

dam

decay *verb*

Decay is used to describe the gradual change of a **radioactive** material. Radioactive **elements**, such as **uranium** and **radium**, set particles of radioactivity free as they decay. This can be used to measure the age of rocks. Decay is also used to describe the process in which dead plants and animals **decompose**.
The amount of the radioactive element decreased as it decayed.

decompose *verb*

Decompose describes the breaking up of a **chemical** into simpler material. When animals and plants die, the complicated **organic** substances of their bodies decompose into simpler substances in the ground.
The dead trees gradually decomposed and became part of the soil.
decomposition *noun*

deep-sea plain ► abyssal plain

degree *noun*

A degree is a unit used for measuring **temperature**. The two common scales for temperature are **Celsius**, or centigrade, and **Fahrenheit**. A degree is also the unit for measuring direction on a **compass** and indicating lines of **latitude** and **longitude**.
Pure water boils at 100 degrees on the Celsius scale.

delta *noun*

A delta is the wide, fan-shaped part of a **river** where it flows into a lake or the sea. The delta is formed by the **sediment** that is carried by the river water. As the river water meets the water of a lake or the sea, the sediment is deposited, often spreading over a large area.
The land in a delta is muddy and very fertile.

deposit *noun*

A deposit is any material that is laid down on a surface as water or other liquids pass. The water in a river leaves a deposit, or **sediment**, of gravel and mud on the river bed.
The water left a deposit of chalk in the kettle.

depression *noun*

A depression is an area of low **atmospheric pressure**. Depressions bring cloudy skies, unsettled weather, and often rain. The opposite of a depression, also called a **cyclone**, is an **anticyclone**. Depression also describes a **hollow** in the ground.
Rain began to fall steadily as the depression arrived.

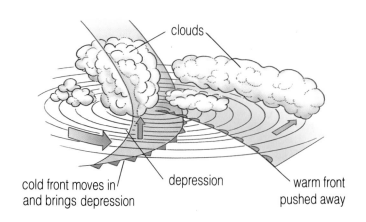

clouds

cold front moves in and brings depression

depression

warm front pushed away

desalination *noun*
Desalination is the process of removing salt from a substance, especially sea water. Desalination takes the salt out of sea water to make it suitable for drinking.
Most of the drinking water in Saudi Arabia is produced by desalination.

desert *noun*
A desert is a dry, open area of land. Deserts usually have less than 10 inches of rain a year. A heavier rainfall that **evaporates** quickly may also occur in a desert. Some deserts, like the Sahara in North Africa, are hot. Other deserts are cold, like the Gobi in eastern Asia. A much smaller range of plants and animals is found in deserts than in other areas, but many kinds of plants and animals are able to survive.
Cactus and other plants have adapted to desert life.

desertification *noun*
Desertification describes how a **desert** spreads. If too many animals living in an area consume all the grass and plants, the soil will suffer from **erosion** and become infertile.
Desertification is increasing the size of the Sahara in North Africa.

detritus *noun*
Detritus is loose, rocky material produced by the **weathering** of exposed rock. Detritus is washed away by rivers and rain and gathers at the bottom of seas, rivers, and lakes, as well as on land.
A thick layer of detritus had been deposited at the edge of the cliff.

Devonian *adjective*
Devonian describes the **period** in **geological time** from about 408 million years ago to 360 million years ago. It was part of the **Paleozoic** Era. (See chart page 64.)
Animals with backbones first came on to the land during the Devonian Period.

dew *noun*
Dew is a collection of water droplets. The droplets **condense** from the water vapor in the air on to the ground, or on to plants. Dew forms at night, when the air cools to below the **dew point**.
In the early morning, the grass was wet with dew.

dew point *noun*
The dew point is the temperature at which **dew** forms from the air. The dew point depends on the dampness of the air and on the **atmospheric pressure**.
The grass became wet as the air cooled and the dew point was reached.

diamond *noun*
Diamond is a shiny, transparent **crystal**. It is a form of **carbon** and is the hardest natural substance known. Colorless diamonds are cut into **gems** for jewelry.
Perfect diamonds are prized for their rarity.

dinosaur *noun*
A dinosaur is any one of a group of reptiles which lived during the **Mesozoic** Era. Dinosaurs lived on Earth for about 140 million years, and died out at the end of the **Cretaceous** Period.
Many dinosaurs walked on two legs.

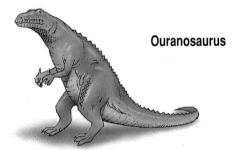

Ouranosaurus

doldrums *noun*
The doldrums describes an area of the **oceans** where the **winds** are often very weak. The doldrums lie a little way north and south of the **Equator**, between the **trade winds**.
Sailing boats are sometimes becalmed in the doldrums.

39

dolerite *noun*
Dolerite is a kind of dark **igneous** rock that contains large amounts of **feldspar**. Dolerite is common all over the world.
Rocks made of dolerite are frequently discovered by hikers.

dolomite *noun*
Dolomite is a **mineral compound** called calcium magnesium carbonate. Dolomite is one of the chief sources of **magnesium**. One kind of **sedimentary** rock that contains calcium magnesium carbonate is also called dolomite. Many mountain ranges, especially in Europe, have huge amounts of dolomite rock.
Weathering has worn the dolomite into jagged cliffs and peaks.

dome *noun*
A dome is a kind of **anticline** in which all the sides slope away evenly from a central point. Domes may be many miles in diameter, or small with steep sides. A dome of impervious rock may act as a trap for **oil** and **natural gas**. A dome can also describe a **hill** with smooth sides. The opposite of a dome is a **basin**.
The slope of the dome provided a gentle climb.

dormant *adjective*
Dormant describes a **volcano** which has not erupted recently but which might erupt again in the future. Volcanoes that erupt are called **active**.
On May 18th, 1980, the dormant volcano of Mount St. Helens erupted in the United States.

drainage *noun*
Drainage describes the way water runs off of soil. If a soil has good drainage, it will dry out quickly after rain. Soil with bad drainage quickly becomes full of water and is difficult to work.
Farmers can improve the drainage by digging ditches below the fields.

drought *noun*
A drought is a long period without rain. Wild plants and animals can often survive short droughts, but crops may suffer badly.
Some areas, such as deserts, often experience droughts.

dune *noun*
A dune is a large hill of **sand** shaped and moved by the wind. Dunes take two main forms, a half-moon or crescent shape, and a narrow ridge shape. Long lines of dunes cover large areas of sandy **deserts**. Dunes are also found near the sea, behind sandy beaches.
It is difficult to walk over soft dunes.

dust *noun*
Dust is a collection of powdery particles of **earth**. In dry weather, dust covers the surface of the soil.
The dust was very fine and was easily blown by the wind.

dust bowl *noun*
The dust bowl is a part of the central plains of the United States. The dust bowl includes the states of Kansas and Texas, which sometimes experience **dust storms**.
In the 1930s, dry weather and storms destroyed much of the farmland of the dust bowl.

dust devil *noun*
A dust devil is a small, circular column of **wind** that has picked up **dust** and soil. A kind of small **tornado** that occurs in dry areas, it can move at a speed of up to 18 miles per hour.
The dust devils looked like moving towers of smoke.

dust storm *noun*
A dust storm is a strong wind that picks up and carries **dust**. Dust storms take place mostly in areas with a hot climate, especially where the soil is fine and dry. Sometimes, small **tornadoes** pick up dust and become dust storms.
The dust storm made driving extremely hazardous.

Earth ► page 42

earth *noun*
Earth is another name for **soil**, the loose material lying above rocks made up of tiny pieces of rock, dust, and sand. These pieces are mixed with **organic** material which has decomposed. (See also pages 42–43.)
When plants grow, they root themselves into the earth.

Earth science *noun*
Earth science is the study of the Earth, including the **oceans** and the **atmosphere**. **Geology**, **meteorology**, glaciology and **oceanography** are all parts of Earth science.
Earth science plays an important role in many industries.

earthquake ► page 46

ebb *verb*
Ebb describes the outward movement of the **tide**. When the tide ebbs, the water in the sea or in an **estuary** moves away from the land. The opposite of ebb is **flow**.
The boat floated out to sea as the tide ebbed.

echo sounder *noun*
An echo sounder measures the distance of an object under water. It sends out sound waves, which bounce back off the seabed, the river bed, or an obstacle under water. The echo sounder calculates depth or distance by measuring the time between sending the sound waves and receiving the echo.
Some fishing boats have echo sounders to help find shoals of fish.

Earth *noun*

The Earth is the planet on which we live. The Earth is made up of several parts. In the center is the **inner core**, which is very dense and may be solid. Around the inner core is the **outer core**, which may be liquid. Both parts of the core are probably made of an **alloy** of iron and nickel. The third layer is the **mantle**, formed from molten rocks. Above the mantle is the **crust**, or **lithosphere**. The outer surface of the crust is covered by land masses such as **continents**, and by **oceans**. Beyond the crust is the **atmosphere**.

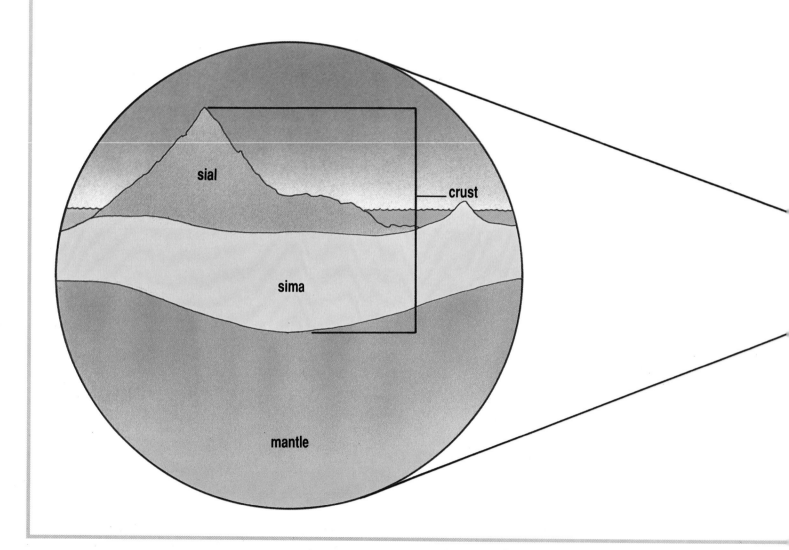

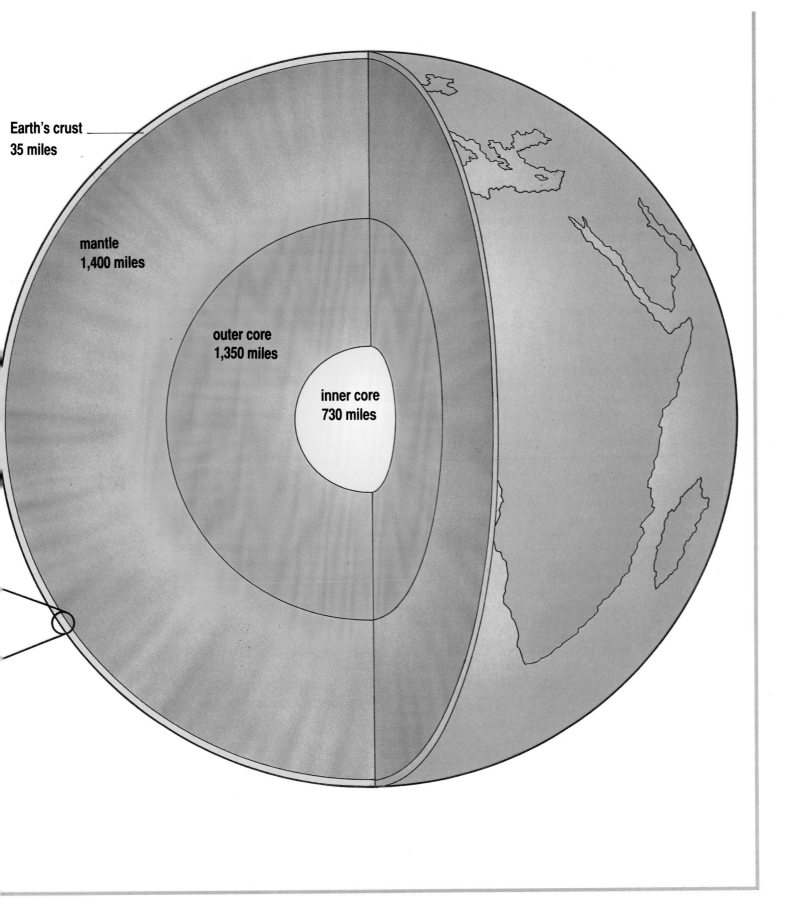

Earth's crust
35 miles

mantle
1,400 miles

outer core
1,350 miles

inner core
730 miles

element *noun*
An element is the most basic substance. An element cannot be changed by chemical reaction into any simpler substance. **Carbon**, **hydrogen**, and **oxygen** are all examples of elements. Elements can join together to form **compounds**. There are just over 100 known elements.
Platinum is a very rare element.

elevation *noun*
Elevation describes the height of an object, usually measured in feet above **sea level**.
The mountain hut was at an elevation of 6,600 feet.

emerald *noun*
Emerald is a green, transparent **crystal**. It is a kind of **beryl**, that contains traces of **chromium**. It is a precious stone.
Emeralds are often used in jewelry.

emery *noun*
Emery is a hard **mineral** that is found in rocks. It is a mixture of **corundum** and oxides of **iron**. Emery is used as an **abrasive** to polish stones, and other surfaces.
Emery feels like sandpaper to the touch.

energy *noun*
Energy is the ability to do work. There are different kinds of energy, including heat energy, light energy, movement or kinetic energy, and chemical energy. Each kind of energy can be changed into another form through chemical or physical means, such as heating.
The waves in the sea contain large amounts of energy.

environment *noun*
The term environment describes our surroundings, or the surroundings of an animal or plant. The environment includes the other animals and plants nearby, as well as the soil, rocks, water, and **climate**.
Changes to the environment can have a great impact on human and animal life.

Eocene *adjective*
Eocene is the **epoch** in **geological time** in the **Tertiary** subera from about 55 million years ago to about 38 million years ago. (See chart page 64.)
The mountains of the Himalayas were formed in the Eocene Epoch.

eon *noun*
An eon is one of the divisions of **geological time**. There are four eons, each covering a very long period of time. The Phanerozoic Eon is the most recent. An eon is divided into **eras**, **periods**, and **epochs**. (See page 64.)
Most forms of life have developed during the Phanerozoic Eon.

epicenter *noun*
The epicenter is the point on the Earth's surface directly above the center, or **focus**, of an **earthquake**. The strongest effects of an earthquake are usually felt at its epicenter.
The city on the epicenter of the earthquake was destroyed.

epoch *noun*
An epoch is one of the divisions of **geological time**. It is a part of a larger division called a **period**. (See chart page 64.)
We live today in the Holocene Epoch.

Equator *noun*
The Equator is an imaginary line that surrounds the **globe**. **Latitude** is measured to the north and south of the Equator, which has latitude 0 degrees. The Equator divides the Earth into two halves, the northern and southern **hemispheres**.
The Sun's heat is most intense near the Equator.

Earth   Equator

44

equatorial   *adjective*
Equatorial refers to the region found near the **Equator**. The equatorial rain forests grow in this region, and the equatorial **current** flows in the seas near the Equator.
The climate is hot in equatorial countries.

era   *noun*
An era is one of the main divisions of **geological time**. Each era is divided into **periods**. The order of eras from oldest to youngest is **Paleozoic**, **Mesozoic**, and **Cenozoic**. (See chart page 64.)
The dinosaurs lived in the Mesozoic Era.

erg   *noun*
An erg is a large area of sand that may be flat or may form sand **dunes**. Ergs are found in **deserts** and can cover huge areas, especially in the Sahara in North Africa.
The camel caravan crossed the erg.

erode   *verb*
To erode is to wear away the surface of something. Wind, water, and ice are constantly eroding the rocks and soils of the Earth.
The rock face was eroded by the wind and rain.

erosion ▶ page 49

erupt   *verb*
A **volcano** erupts when it explodes. Dormant volcanoes may not erupt for many years, or even centuries. Other volcanoes erupt more frequently.
We dared not go too near the volcano, in case it erupted.

eruption   *noun*
An eruption is the explosion of a **volcano**. In an eruption, a volcano spouts out ash and red-hot **lava**, which flows down the sides of the volcano.
The eruption destroyed every living thing on the sides of the volcano.

escarpment   *noun*
An escarpment is a steep slope rising up from a **plain**. An escarpment is formed when the rocks are **eroded** much more quickly on one side of a hill than at the other.
The escarpment blocked the route out of the valley.

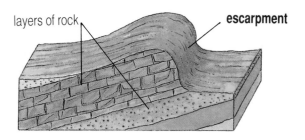
layers of rock   escarpment

esker   *noun*
An esker is a long, narrow hill or **ridge**, winding along a **valley** floor. Eskers are created by streams flowing underneath **glaciers**. The streams leave behind **sand** and **gravel**, which form the esker.
The road followed the top of the esker.

estuary   *noun*
An estuary is the part of a **river** where fresh water flows into the sea. The fresh river water mixes with the salty sea water. An estuary is affected by the **tides**. The water in the parts of the river nearest the sea rises and falls as the tide **ebbs** and **flows**.
Many seaports are built on estuaries.

earthquake *noun*

An earthquake is a large, sudden movement of the Earth's **crust**. The crust is divided into several **tectonic plates**. The edges of the plates are marked by **faults**. When the plates move past each other, or collide, earthquakes can occur along the fault lines. The strength of an earthquake is measured on the **Mercalli Scale**, or more often, the **Richter Scale**.

Strong earthquakes may cause great damage and loss of life.

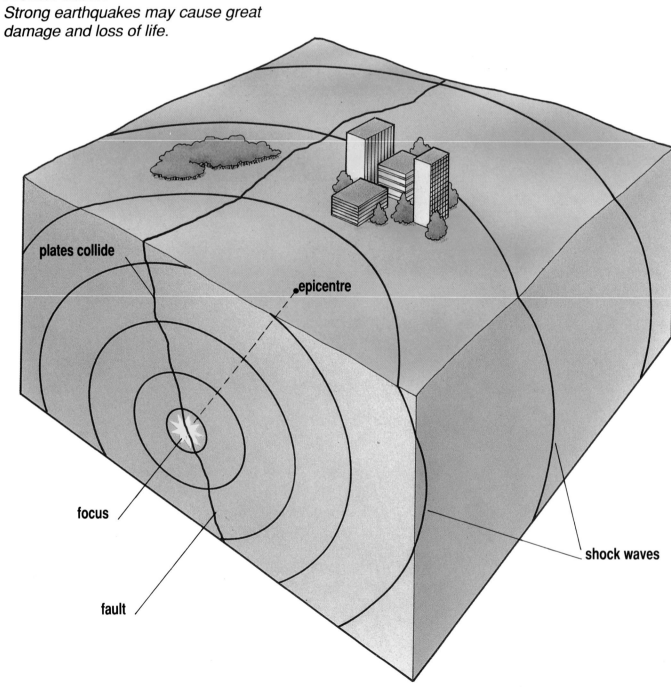

plates collide

epicentre

focus

fault

shock waves

types of fault

normal fault

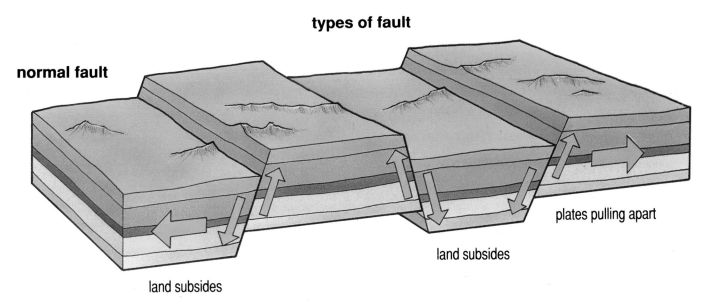

plates pulling apart

land subsides

land subsides

reverse fault

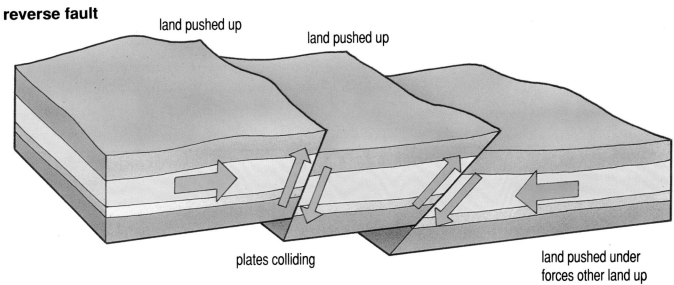

land pushed up

land pushed up

plates colliding

land pushed under
forces other land up

transcurrent fault

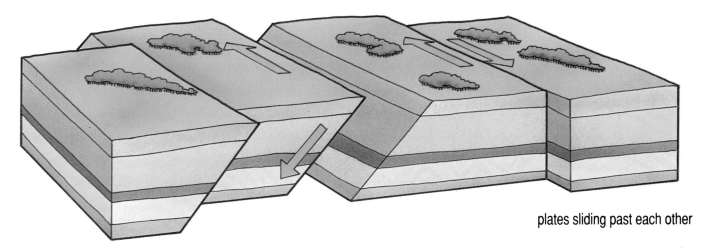

plates sliding past each other

evaporate   *verb*
Evaporate describes how a liquid changes into a **gas** or **vapor**. Water evaporates when it is heated, turning from a liquid into water **vapor** in the air.
The water in the vase evaporated in the heat of the Sun.

evaporation   *noun*
Evaporation describes the process in which a liquid turns into a **gas**. Water turns into water **vapor** in the air as it evaporates from oceans, lakes, rivers, and soil.
The level of water in the small lake fell because of evaporation.

excavate   *verb*
To excavate is to dig carefully. Geologists excavate **quarries** and **cliffs** when looking for **fossils** or **minerals**.
The team excavated the area looking for dinosaur bones.
excavation   *noun*

extinct   *adjective*
Extinct describes a **volcano** that has not **erupted** for a long time and that is not expected to erupt again. The opposite of an extinct volcano is an **active** volcano. Extinct also describes an organism which is no longer living.
Trees had grown along the slope of the extinct volcano.

extract   *verb*
To extract something is to take it out. **Metals** are extracted from their **ores** by melting or by the use of **chemicals**.
The miners extracted pure gold from the rocks.

extraction   *noun*
Extraction describes how one substance is taken out of a mixture. Extraction can be performed by heating and melting the mixture, or by dissolving the mixture in **chemicals**.
Metals are taken from their ores by the process of extraction.

extreme   *adjective*
Extreme describes something that is beyond the usual known range. An extreme **temperature** is a very hot or a very cold temperature.
They were forced to take shelter from the extreme heat of the desert.

eye   *noun*
Eye is sometimes used to describe the central part of a storm of circular winds or **hurricane**. The air in the area of the eye is calm.
The eye of the storm was surrounded by fierce, swirling winds.

erosion *noun*

Erosion is the wearing down of **rocks** or **soils**, caused by the action of **water**, **wind**, or **ice**, or by living organisms. The force of sea water washing against cliffs will erode the cliffs, breaking down the solid rock into smaller pieces. Further erosion will turn boulders and pebbles into sand. Many interesting **rock formations** and **features** are caused by erosion.

The headlands at each end of the bay were eroded by the sea into a range of sea cliffs.

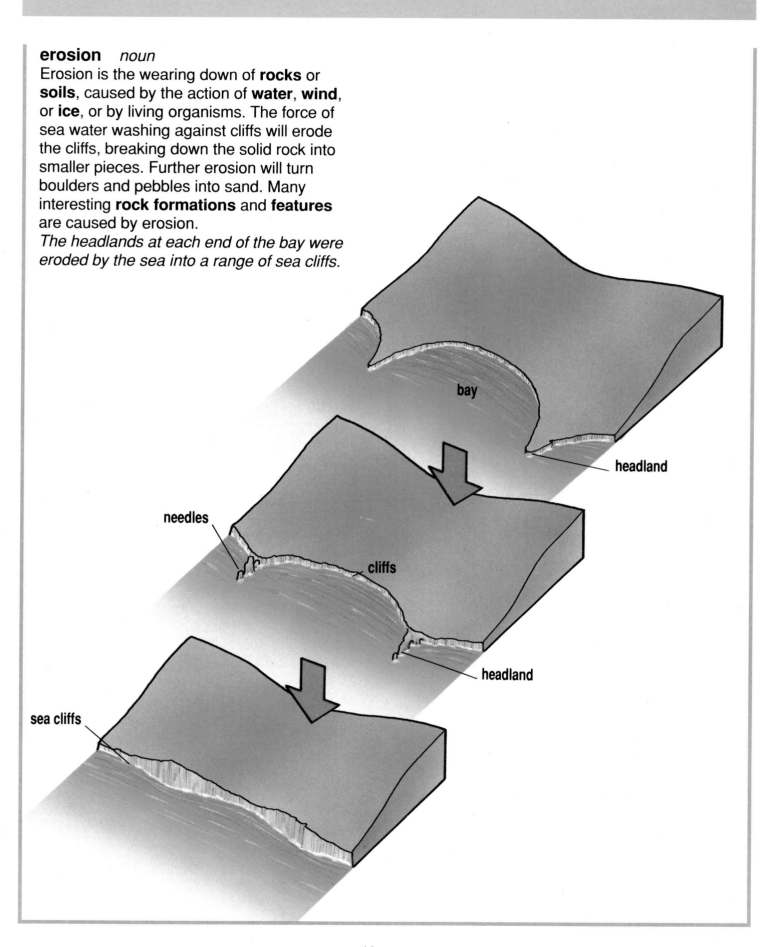

49

facet *noun*
As a precious stone or **gem** used for jewelry is cut into several flat surfaces, each of these flat surfaces is called a facet.
Each facet of the diamond shone as it caught the light.

facet

Fahrenheit *noun*
Fahrenheit is a scale used for measuring **temperature**. On the Fahrenheit scale, the freezing point of water is 32 degrees and the boiling point is 212 degrees. Temperature is more often measured on the **Celsius scale**.
The daily temperature is measured on the Fahrenheit scale in the United States.

fault *noun*
A fault is a crack in rocks, caused by movements of the Earth's **crust**. Faults can make the ground crack, and bend, sometimes creating **valleys** and **cliffs**.
One of the most famous faults is the San Andreas Fault in California, in the United States.

feature ► page 52

feldspar *noun*
Feldspar is a kind of **mineral** made up of **crystals**. It contains **aluminum** and **silica**, with mixtures of **sodium**, **potassium**, and **calcium**.
Nearly half of all the rocks in the Earth's crust are feldspar.

fen *noun*
A fen is a kind of wetland. In a fen, the water has a high **mineral** content, and the main plants are sedges and grasses. Fens often develop at the edges of **lowland** lakes.
Fens are characteristic of the English landscape.

ferrous *adjective*
Ferrous describes something, such as metal, that is made of the metal **iron**, or that contains iron.
Steel is an example of a ferrous metal.

fertile *adjective*
Fertile describes something that can support growth. Healthy plants grow in a fertile soil. Fertile also describes an animal or plant that can produce young or seeds.
The farmer grew good crops in the fertile soil.

fertilizer *noun*
Fertilizer is a **chemical** or mixture of chemicals added to soil to make it more **fertile**. Compost and manure are forms of natural ferilizer.
Most fertilizers contain nitrogen, which is beneficial to plant life.

fissure *noun*
A fissure is a long and narrow cleft or crack in a rock or in the soil. Fissures develop when the ground splits or when rock is worn away by water. They are common in **volcanic** areas.
We could see the steam rising from the fissure in the rock.

fjord   *noun*

A fjord is a deep **inlet** of the sea with steep mountain slopes on each side. They were formed when the sea flooded river valleys caused by glaciers. Fjords are found on hilly or mountainous **coasts**.

The coasts of Norway and of the South Island of New Zealand have many fjords.

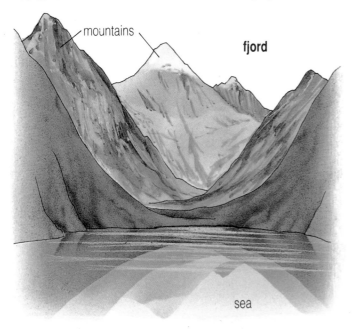

flash flood   *noun*

A flash flood is a **flood** that occurs very suddenly. Flash floods occur mainly in warm countries, especially where the rocks are **impervious** and water cannot drain away. They can destroy crops and cause **erosion**.

The flash flood washed away the soil.

flint   *noun*

Flint is a hard rock found as gray or brown **pebbles** in **chalk** or **limestone**.

In the Stone Age, early humans made tools by breaking the flint into pieces with sharp edges.

flood   *noun*

A flood is a sudden rise in **water level** covering land that is usually dry. Floods may happen on low-lying land near the **coast** when there are high **tides** and strong winds. *Heavy rainfall can cause a flood by raising the water level of a river over its banks.*

flood plain   *noun*

A flood plain is the flat valley floor that fills with water when a **lowland** river floods. A flood plain usually has very **fertile** soil made of **sediment** deposited by the river when it floods.

The river flowed in many meanders along the flood plain.

flora   *noun*

Flora is used to describe all of the plants of a particular region or a particular time. The tropical **rain forests** have the richest flora on Earth.

The flora of the northeastern United States is able to survive harsh winters.

flow   *verb*

Flow describes the inward movement of the **tide**. When the tide flows, the water in the sea or in an **estuary** moves toward the land. The opposite of flow is **ebb**.

The captain had to wait until the tide began to flow before his boat could sail.

fluorine   *noun*

The **element** fluorine is a yellow **gas** found naturally in the mineral **fluorite**. Sodium fluoride is a fluorine **compound** that is sometimes added to drinking water to help teeth to grow strong.

Fluorine forms compounds with nearly all other elements.

fluorite   *noun*

Fluorite is a **mineral** with a white or purple color found mainly in mineral **veins**. Fluorite is made of calcium fluoride and is the main source of **fluorine**.

The scientists found fluorite in the quarry.

feature *noun*

A feature is a distinctive part of the **landscape**. In a flat **plain**, a steep **cliff** is be a feature in the landscape. Some features, such as the ones below, are so unusual that they are famous all over the world.

The huge rock formations were the main feature of the valley.

Rainbow Bridge in Utah, was formed by water eroding sandstone.

Strange piles of rock can sometimes be found in the ergs in the Sahara in North Africa.

This red sandstone butte is in Monument Valley in the state of Utah.

Houses have been built into these volcanic rock formations in Cappadocia, Turkey.

Ayers Rock, or Uluru, is a partly buried mass of sandstone in Northern Territory, Australia. It is over 1.8 miles long.

These limstone rock formations are in the Band-i-Amir River in the Hindu Kush mountains of Afghanistan.

These six-sided basalt columns are part of the Giant's Causeway in County Antrim, Northern Ireland.

focus *noun*
The focus is the point below the Earth's surface where an **earthquake** begins. The point on the surface of the Earth directly above the focus is called the **epicenter** of the earthquake.
The focus of the earthquake was deep below the Earth's surface.

fog *noun*
Fog is used to describe thick **clouds** formed at ground level. Fog develops when water **vapor** in the air cools below the **dew point**.
The fog was so thick that they could not see the road ahead.

fold *noun*
A fold is a bend in a layer of rocks. Folds are found most commonly in **sedimentary** and **metamorphic** rocks. A fold that is arch-shaped is called an **anticline**. A fold that is trough-shaped is a **syncline**.
The colored bands in the rock showed the fold clearly.

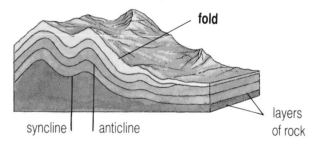

fold

syncline   anticline

layers of rock

fold mountain *noun*
A fold mountain is a mountain formed from a **fold** in the rocks. The mountains of Scotland, Wales, and Norway are fold mountains, as are the Himalayas in Asia and the Pyrenees in Europe.
The long chain of fold mountains stretched into the distance.

ford *noun*
A ford is the place where a road crosses a **stream** or a **river**. The water is usually shallow and the bed of the river is firm.
We walked beside the stream until we could cross it at the ford.

forecast *noun*
A forecast predicts events in the future. The **weather forecast** gives information about future weather. The shipping forecast provides details of the weather at sea.
He listened to the weather forecast before setting out.

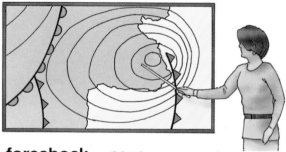

foreshock *noun*
Foreshock is the shock or **tremor** that occurs a short time before an **earthquake**.
The foreshock before the earthquake was barely noticeable.

forest *noun*
A forest is a large area of woodland. Many forests grow naturally and may be hundreds of years old. Some forests are carefully planted and the wood, a **natural resource**, is cut at intervals.
In northern Europe, dark, coniferous forests stretch for hundreds of miles.

forestry *noun*
Forestry is the study and care of growing and developing **forests**. A forester may look after trees being grown especially for timber, as well as caring for natural forests.
Advances in forestry are applied to maintain healthy stands of trees .

fossil ► page 56

fossil fuel *noun*
Fossil fuel describes fuel that has formed from the fossilized remains of plants. **Peat**, **coal**, and **natural gas** are all fossil fuels. Fossil fuels contain **carbon** and are a good source of **energy** when burned.
When they are used, fossil fuels are not replenishable.

fracture *noun*
A fracture is an area in the Earth's surface where the rocks have moved apart. Many fractures are found beside the **midoceanic ridges** at the bottom of the sea.
The fracture in the rocks was caused by an earthquake.

freeze-thaw *adjective*
Freeze-thaw describes a kind of **weathering**. In freeze-thaw weathering, the water in rocks or soils freezes and then thaws repeatedly. Water expands when it freezes, so it enlarges any cracks in the rocks. Freeze-thaw action is most common during cold weather in high mountains, and in the **polar** regions.
The rocks were covered in tiny cracks caused by freeze-thaw action.

fresh water *noun*
Fresh water is the water usually found in the ground and in rivers and lakes. Unlike sea water, fresh water does not have a high salt content and is easily turned into drinking water.
At the top of an estuary, the water changes from salt water to fresh water.

front *noun*
A front describes a sharp change in the **temperature** of air. A **warm front** occurs at the edge of a mass of warm air and a **cold front** is found at the edge of a mass of cold air. Fronts also separate water masses of different temperatures in the **ocean**.
The weather suddenly became milder as the warm front arrived.

frontier *noun*
A frontier is an imaginary line that separates one country from another. The frontier is also the part of a country that faces, or fronts, another country or the less developed outer areas. Some frontiers are marked by a fence or a wall. Some are formed by natural barriers, such as mountains or rivers.
Travel can become more difficult as one approaches the frontier.

frost *noun*
Frost occurs when the air or ground **temperature** is so cold that **ice** forms. Moisture in the air or on the ground **condenses** and then freezes on the soil and on plants.
A severe frost can kill delicate plants.

fuel *noun*
Fuel is any substance that is used to produce **energy**. **Coal**, **gas**, and **oil** are fuels that are burned to obtain heat. Petroleum is another fuel, which is made from **crude oil**. Nuclear power stations use **radioactive chemicals** as fuel, usually a form of **uranium**.
Scientists continue to seek new ways to use fuel efficiently.

fumarole *noun*
A fumarole is a small hole in the Earth's surface through which steam and **gases** escape. Fumaroles are found in **volcanic** areas. The steam comes from water heated by **magma** under the ground. **Dormant** volcanoes sometimes have many fumaroles.
Hot steam rose out of the fumarole.

funnel *noun*
A funnel is a circular opening in rocks, which is wide at the top and narrow at the bottom. Funnels often occur in **caves**.
The funnel in the rocks had been caused by erosion.

fossil *noun*

A fossil is the remains of an organism that lived on Earth in an earlier **geological time**. Fossils are usually found in **sedimentary** rocks. The study of fossils is called **paleontology**.

The ammonite fossil was embedded in the limestone.

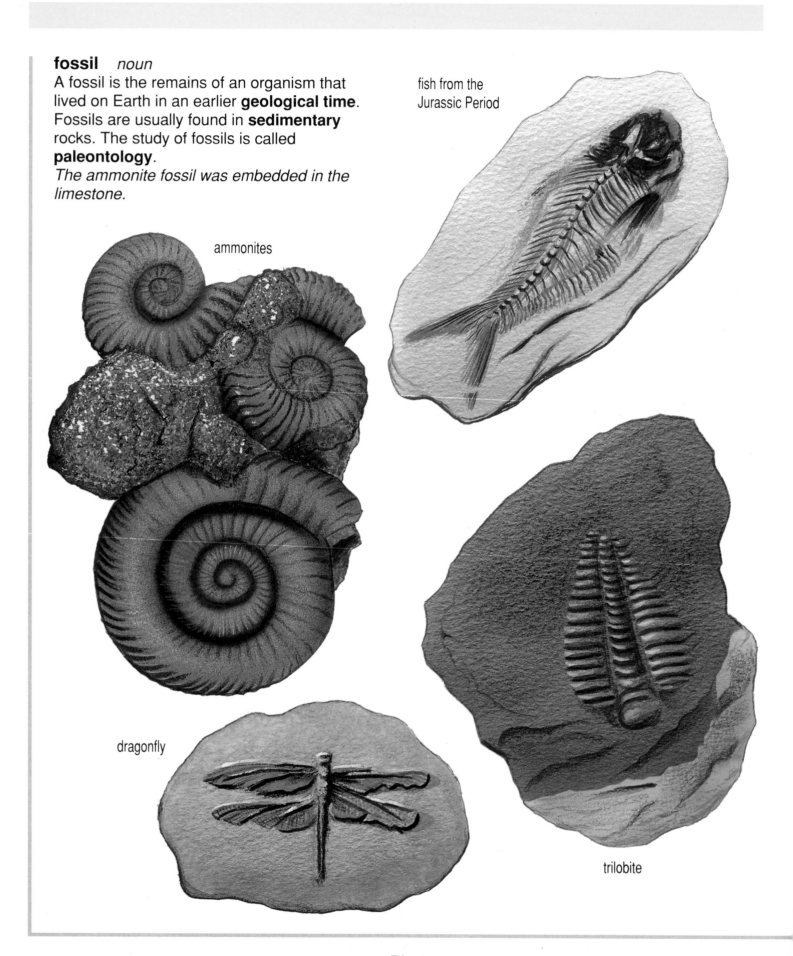

fish from the Jurassic Period

ammonites

dragonfly

trilobite

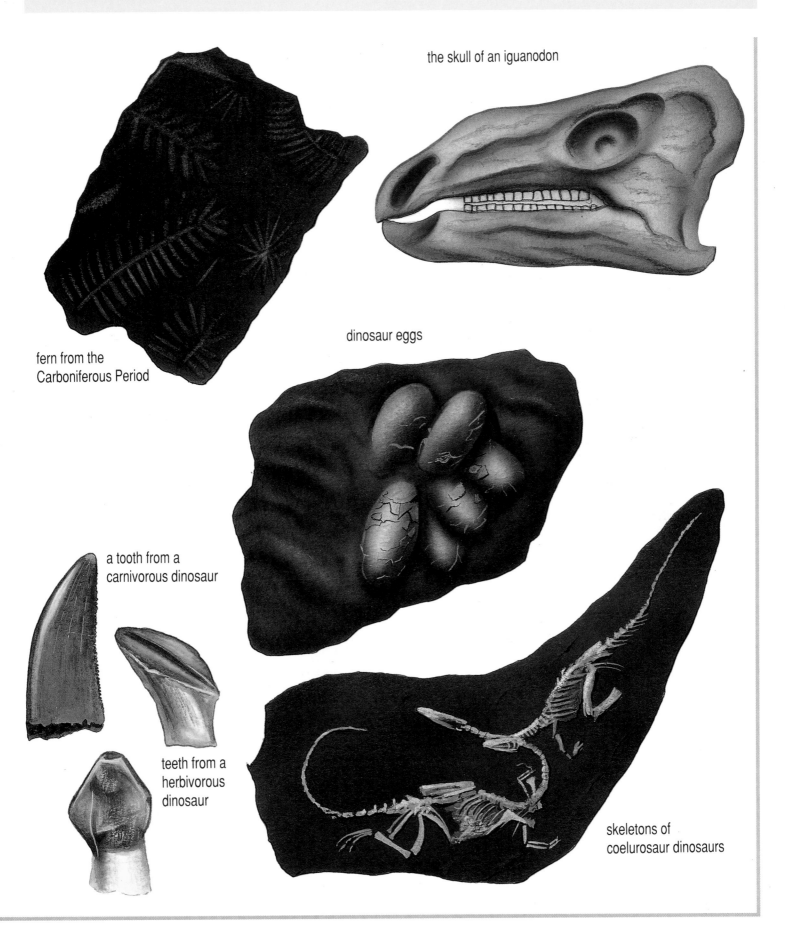

the skull of an iguanodon

fern from the
Carboniferous Period

dinosaur eggs

a tooth from a
carnivorous dinosaur

teeth from a
herbivorous
dinosaur

skeletons of
coelurosaur dinosaurs

gale   *noun*
A gale is a very strong **wind**. It can break twigs from trees, and even damage buildings. A gale measures between forces 7 and 9 on the **Beaufort Scale**.
The gale blew so hard that we found it difficult to walk upright.

galena   *noun*
Galena is a **mineral** made of dark gray crystals of **lead** sulfide. Galena is the most important source of the metal lead.
The miners found large deposits of galena in the rocks.

garnet   *noun*
Garnet describes a group of **minerals** found mostly in **metamorphic** rocks. Garnet crystals are made of **silicates** of **magnesium**, **aluminum**, **iron**, and **calcium**. Dark red garnets are used as **gems**.
A garnet can be used as an abrasive.

gas   *noun*
A gas is one of the three types of matter. The molecules in a gas are very active and are well spread out. Gases have low densities and can be compressed. They can also flow freely.
Air is a mixture of gases, mostly nitrogen and oxygen.

gaseous   *adjective*
Gaseous describes a substance when it is a **gas**. All substances change to a gaseous form when they reach a high enough **temperature**.
Water vapor is the gaseous form of water.

gem   ► page 60

geo-   *prefix*
Geo- is a prefix used to refer to the **Earth**.
Geology is the study of the Earth's rocks and minerals.

geochemistry   *noun*
Geochemistry is the study of the chemical **elements** that are found on **Earth**. It includes studying the chemical processes involved in the Earth's history.
The study of geochemistry helps scientists to find mineral deposits.

geode   *noun*
A geode is a hollow space completely surrounded by rock. Geodes are found in **igneous** rocks. They are partly filled by mineral **crystals** that face inward.
The geologist found a patch of shiny crystals hidden inside the geode.

geodesy   *noun*
Geodesy is the study of the size and shape of the **Earth** and its field of **gravity**. In geodesy, scientists measure the Earth's curve.
Geodesy plays an important role in the planning of space missions.

geographer   *noun*
A geographer is someone who studies or practices **geography**.
A geographer must be aware of the changes in the Earth's features.

geography *noun*
Geography is the study of the **Earth's** surface. Physical geography includes the Earth's **climate**, **vegetation**, and **oceans**. Human geography looks at the peoples of the world and their **environments**. Mathematical geography studies the size, shape, and movements of the Earth.
We learned about the main features of the North American continent in geography.

geological time ► page 64

geologist *noun*
A geologist is someone who studies or practices **geology**.
The geologist studied the rocks and minerals of the cliff.

geology *noun*
Geology is the study of the **Earth**. Different branches of geology deal with the Earth's history, the movements that take place within it, the materials it is made from, and the shapes of these materials. Geology also studies the plants and animals that have lived on Earth throughout the different ages.
Geology often involves trips into the field.

geomagnetism *noun*
Geomagnetism is the **magnetism** of the **Earth**. It is caused by the metals at the **core** of the Earth, which act like a huge **magnet**. These metals, which are mainly **iron** and **nickel**, set up a **magnetic field** around the Earth.
The needle of a compass is sensitive to geomagnetism.

geomorphology *noun*
Geomorphology is the branch of **geology** that studies the structure of the **Earth's** surface. Geomorphology looks at such changes as **erosion** and the laying down of **deposits**.
Geomorphology could determine how long it had taken the rocks to wear away.

geophysics *noun*
Geophysics is a branch of **geology**. Geophysics looks at the physical properties of the **Earth** and at the forces that shape it.
The study of the Earth's magnetic field is a part of geophysics.

geothermal energy *noun*
Geothermal energy is **energy** that comes from the heat of the Earth's rocks. In some areas, geothermal energy is used for heating water and for making electricity.
Every room in the house was heated by geothermal energy.

geyser *noun*
A geyser is a fountain of hot water and steam found in **volcanic** areas. Geysers only spout at intervals, when hot water and **gases** build up underground.
The world's most famous geyser is Old Faithful in Yellowstone National Park, in the United States.

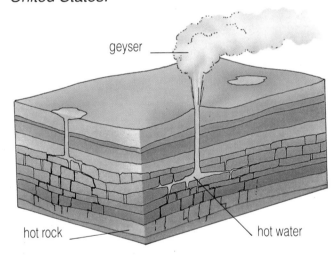

glaciation *noun*
Glaciation is the way in which land is shaped by **ice**. Thick layers of ice move slowly over hills and mountains while the ice gouges out the soil and rocks. Glaciation is also the name for the periods in geological history when ice covered the Earth.
The sides of the valley had been worn smooth during the last glaciation.

glacier ► page 66

gem *noun*

A gem is any precious or semiprecious **mineral**. Gems may be many different colors, including red rubies, green emeralds, or blue sapphires.

Most gems and crystals sparkle when they are cut and polished.

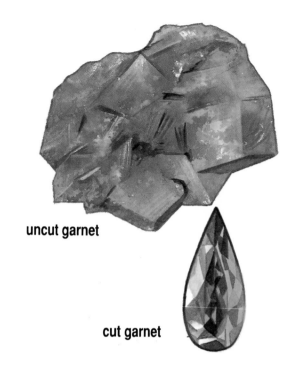

uncut garnet

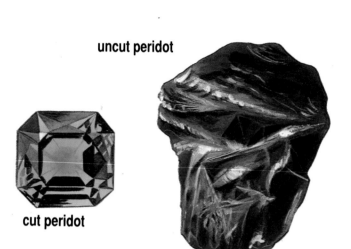

uncut peridot

cut peridot

cut garnet

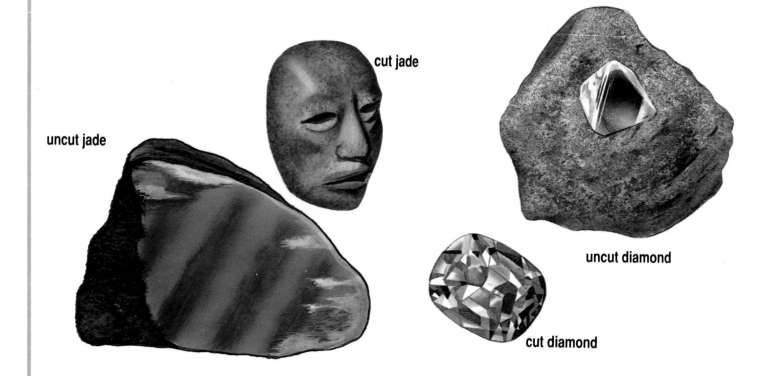

cut jade

uncut jade

uncut diamond

cut diamond

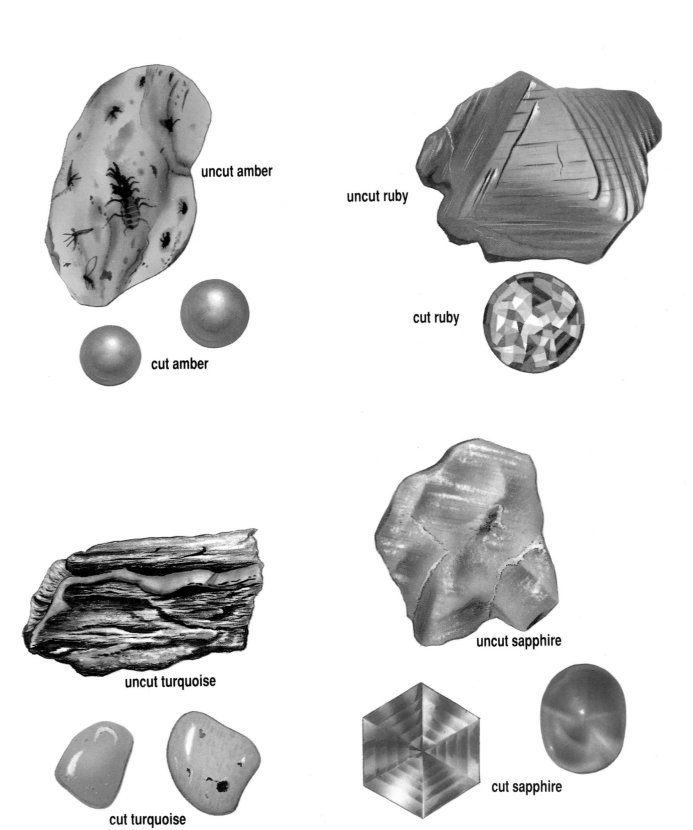

uncut amber

cut amber

uncut ruby

cut ruby

uncut turquoise

cut turquoise

uncut sapphire

cut sapphire

glass *noun*
Glass is a clear substance made from **lime**, soda, and **silica**. Glass turns liquid when it is heated. Liquid glass can be molded or blown into different shapes. Elements, such as **boron** and **lead**, are added to glass to give it special properties. Glass occurs naturally as **obsidian**.
We could see the fish clearly in the glass tank.

global *adjective*
Global describes something that affects the whole **Earth**. An animal or plant that is found throughout the world has a global distribution. Global warming heats up the **climate** of the whole Earth.
The astronauts had a global view of Earth from their spacecraft.

globe *noun*
The globe is the name given to the planet **Earth**.
The spacecraft circled the globe.

gneiss *noun*
Gneiss is a kind of **metamorphic** rock made up of coarse **crystals** arranged in light and dark colored bands. The largest areas of gneiss in the world are in central Australia, Canada, and the Baltic region of northern Europe.
The rocky hills were formed of gneiss.

gold *noun*
Gold is an **element**. It is a soft, bright yellow **metal** that does not react easily with other **chemicals**. Gold is rare and valuable.
Gold is used for making some coins, jewelery and ornaments.

Gondwanaland *noun*
Gondwanaland is the name of a large **continent** which some scientists think formed when **Pangaea** split up about 215 million years ago, during the **Mesozoic** Era. Gondwanaland may also have split, to create South America, Antarctica, Africa, India, Australia and New Zealand. (See illustration page 108.)
Some scientists think Gondwanaland was formed in the southern hemisphere.

gorge *noun*
A gorge is a very deep **valley** with steep sides. Most gorges have fast rivers flowing through them. Large gorges are sometimes called **canyons**.
The river flowed through the narrow gorge.

gradient *noun*
A gradient is a measure of **slope**. High up a hill or mountain, the gradient usually becomes steeper.
The mountain became more difficult to climb as the gradient increased.

granite *noun*
Granite is a kind of **igneous** rock or stone. Granite is hard, with a coarse grain and a pink or gray color. Granite is a mixture of **feldspar**, **quartz**, and **mica**.
The building was made entirely of granite.

graphite *noun*
Graphite is a **mineral** found in **metamorphic** rocks. It is a soft, dark gray form of pure **carbon**. It can be used to conduct heat. Graphite is slippery and can also be used as a lubricant.
The leads used in pencils are made from graphite mixed with clay.

grassland *noun*
A grassland is a region where grass is the main kind of plant. Large grasslands are found in East Africa and in parts of central Asia. Grasslands occur where there is not enough **rainfall** for trees to grow well.
The grassland was plowed up to grow crops.

gravel *noun*
Gravel is small pieces of rock, which range in size from a sixth to a twelfth of an inch. Gravel is between **sand** and **pebbles** in size.
Some deserts are made up of gravel and small stones.

gravity *noun*
Gravity is a force that pulls objects toward the center of the **Earth**. Gravity is also the force that gives the **planets** a regular movement around the Sun.
The force of gravity is observed any time an object falls to the floor when it is dropped.
gravitate *verb*

greenhouse effect *noun*
The greenhouse effect is a theory that describes the gradual warming of the **atmosphere** of the **Earth**. The greenhouse effect is thought to be caused by the build-up of **carbon dioxide** and **methane** in the atmosphere. These gases prevent heat escaping from the Earth's surface and the lower part of the atmosphere.
Some scientists think that the greenhouse effect will cause average temperatures to rise by between 1 and 5 degrees Celsius by the year 2050.

Greenwich meridian *noun*
The Greenwich meridian is an imaginary vertical line on the Earth's surface. It joins the **North Pole** and **South Pole** and crosses the **Equator** at a right angle. **Meridians** are a measure of **longitude**. The Greenwich meridian is 0 degrees longitude and all the other meridians are measured in **degrees** from the Greenwich meridian. The meridian takes its name from Greenwich in the British Isles, through which it passes.
Sailors constantly mark their position against the location of Greenwich meridian.

grid *noun*
A grid is a system of two sets of lines that cross each other. The lines that make up the grid around the **Earth** are called lines of **longitude** and lines of **latitude**. A numbered grid is used on **maps**, where horizontal and vertical grid numbers show the position of a place.
We reached the lake by following the grid on the map.

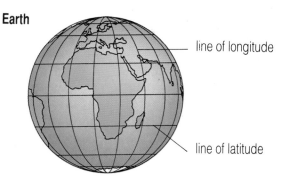

Earth — line of longitude — line of latitude

grotto *noun*
A grotto is a kind of **cave**. Grottoes are common in **limestone** areas where water has worn away the rock.
The river flowed into a large, dark grotto.

ground *noun*
Ground is a word used to describe the surface of the **land**. In rocky areas, the ground is very hard, while it can be soft and soggy in **marshes**, **bogs**, and **fens**.
It was easy to build the house because the ground was firm and level.

geological time *noun*

Geological time is the system geologists use to divide up the Earth's known history. The largest divisions are the four **eons**. The most recent eon is divided into three **eras**. The eras are divided in turn into **periods**. The three most recent periods are split into seven **epochs**.

Eons are all part of geological time.

Priscoan Eon	Archean Eon
4,600 millions of years ago	4,000

oldest rock

first evidence of life

3,950   3,500

Phanerozoic Eon

Paleozoic Era

Cambrian Period	Ordovician Period	Silurian Period	Devonian Period	Carboniferous Pe
590 millions of years ago	505	438	408	360
first trilobites appear	fish first appear	land plants first appear	amphibians first appear	reptiles first appear
570	450	400	365	338

Precambrian

Proterozoic Eon

2,500	590
	millions of years ago

true
plants
first
appear

1,350

	Mesozoic Era			Cenozoic Era						
				Tertiary subera					Quaternary subera	
Permian Period	Triassic Period	Jurassic Period	Cretaceous Period	Paleogene Period			Neogene Period		Pleistogene Period	
286	248	213	144	65	55	38	24½	5	2 people first appear	1/100
	mammals first appear	birds first appear		Paleocene Epoch	Eocene Epoch	Oligocene Epoch	Miocene Epoch	Pliocene Epoch	Pleistocene Epoch	Holocene Epoch
		200	150						2	

glacier *noun*

A glacier is a river of **ice**, **rocks**, and **soil**. It is formed from densely packed **snow**, called **névé**, that never melts. Névé is pressed down so hard that it turns to ice. The pressure eventually forces the ice to move downhill. Most glaciers move only an inch or two a day. Some steep glaciers make creaking noises. Glaciers are found in high mountains and also in Antarctica.
Scientists study glaciers to learn about Ice Ages in the Earth's past.

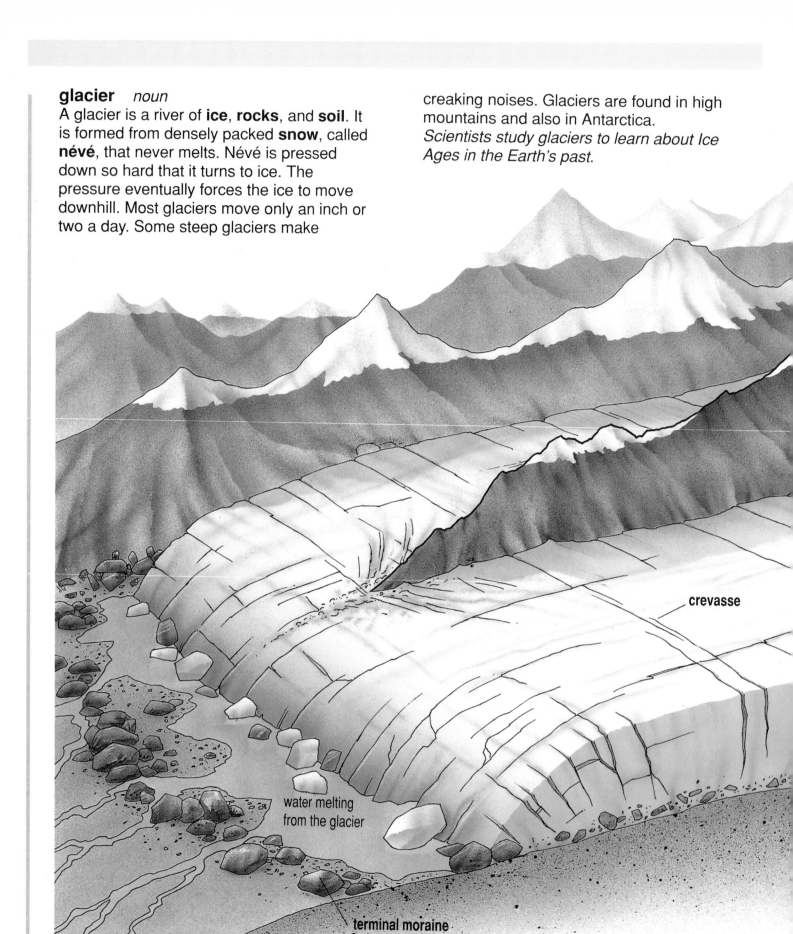

crevasse

water melting from the glacier

terminal moraine

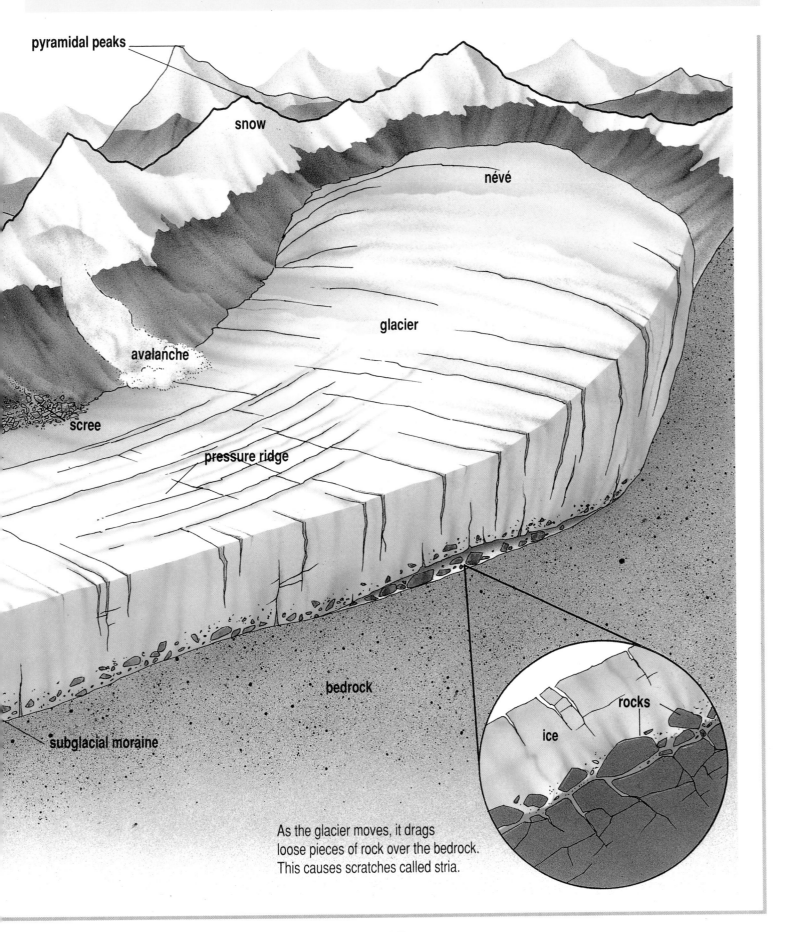

pyramidal peaks

snow

névé

glacier

avalanche

scree

pressure ridge

bedrock

subglacial moraine

rocks

ice

As the glacier moves, it drags
loose pieces of rock over the bedrock.
This causes scratches called stria.

ground frost   *noun*
Ground frost describes a **frost** that only freezes the surface of the **ground**. A ground frost is a light frost that usually does little damage to growing plants.
The weather forecast predicted a ground frost overnight.

ground water   *noun*
Ground water is water that soaks into **porous** rocks in the ground. **Springs** develop where there are rocks full of ground water at the surface of the Earth.
A deep well was sunk in the porous rocks to pump up the ground water.

gulf   *noun*
A gulf is a large area of sea that is almost enclosed by land. The large Persian Gulf lies between Iran and Saudi Arabia in the Middle East.
The ships sailed into the more sheltered waters of the gulf.

gully   *noun*
A gully is a narrow **channel** in rock or soil. Gullies are usually formed by **erosion**. Water may make a gully by wearing away soft earth or rock.
The stream had worn away a gully in the mud of the salt marsh.

gypsum   *noun*
Gypsum is a **mineral** made of calcium sulfate. Gypsum is found naturally either as **crystals** or as a fine-grained substance called **alabaster**.
Plaster of Paris is made from gypsum.

gyre   *noun*
A gyre is the circular movement of water. In some parts of the sea, the **currents** move in a gyre.
The ocean currents moved slowly around in the gyre.

68

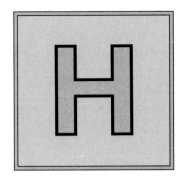

hail *noun*

Hail is frozen raindrops. The pieces of **ice** in hail are called hailstones. Hailstones may be as large as 2 inches in diameter.
The entire crop was flattened by the hailstorm.

hamada *noun*

A hamada is a kind of **desert** where the surface of the ground is bare rock. Wind has swept away any loose material, and polished the rock's surface.
There are areas of hamada in the Sahara in North Africa.

hanging valley *noun*

A hanging valley is a geological **feature**. A hanging valley meets a larger **valley** at a point high up on the side of the larger valley. Hanging valleys were formed by the action of **glaciers**.
The hanging valley lay at the top of a steep slope.

hard water *noun*

Hard water is water that contains large amounts of dissolved **calcium** and **magnesium** salts. Hard water is often found in **limestone** areas.
The hard water left a layer of calcium in the water pipes.

haze *noun*

Haze describes a very thin **mist**. It also describes the effect of warm **air** rising through cooler air, which is called a heat haze.
It was difficult to see the city skyline clearly because of the haze.

headland *noun*

A headland is a narrow piece of land jutting out into the **sea**. Headlands often end in **cliffs** that fall steeply to the sea. Many lighthouses are built on headlands.
The boat came into view as it rounded the headland.

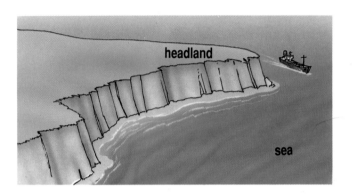

heat *noun*

Heat is the **energy** we feel when the **temperature** of an object or substance increases. Heat is given out when **fuel** is burned. The Sun also gives out heat, which warms the surface of the Earth. Heat is measured in units called joules.
They had to shade themselves from the heat of the desert sun.

heavy mineral *noun*

A heavy mineral is a mineral that has a large mass. When it is a powder, it will sink in a liquid. **Zircon** and **iron** are heavy minerals.
The geologist separated the heavy minerals from the solution.

hectare *noun*

A hectare is a metric unit of measurement that measures area. One hectare is equal to 10,000 square meters (1 square meter = 1.2 square yards).
The trees covered about 5 hectares.

helium *noun*

Helium is an **element**, a very light **gas**. Helium is an **inert** gas, so it does not react with other elements.
Helium is used to fill balloons and blimps.

hematite   *noun*
Hematite is a **mineral** found in **igneous** rocks and also in some types of **sandstone**. It is a kind of **iron** oxide and has a reddish color.
Hematite is used as an ore in the production of iron.

hemisphere   *noun*
Hemisphere describes one half of the **globe**. The northern and southern hemispheres are separated by the **Equator**.
There is more land in the northern hemisphere than in the southern hemisphere.

high pressure   *noun*
High pressure is an area of the air where the **atmospheric pressure** is high. It is also known as an **anticyclone** and is the opposite of a **depression**. High pressure areas usually bring clear, dry weather.
The clouds disappeared as the high pressure system arrived.

hill   *noun*
A hill is a high area of the **landscape** with a definite **summit**. Hills rise up from the surrounding **lowland**. Some hills are single and others are found in **ranges**. Hills can vary in size from several feet high to two thousand feet or so. A hill is not as high as a **mountain**.
The village lay at the bottom of the hill.

hoarfrost   *noun*
Hoarfrost is a kind of frost that is produced when the air near the ground cools down very fast at night. Hoarfrost coats the grass and trees with **crystals** of **ice**.
In the morning, the hoarfrost sparkled in the garden.

hollow   *noun*
A hollow is a shallow dip in the surface of the ground. Some hollows form when the ground below collapses. Other hollows are caused by the action of ice.
There was a small lake at the bottom of the hollow.

Holocene   *adjective*
Holocene describes the most recent **epoch** in **geological time**. It began about 10,000 years ago and continues today. The word Holocene means recent. (See chart page 64.)
Mammoths died out just before the Holocene Epoch.

horizon   *noun*
Horizon describes a horizontal **layer**, or **stratum**, either in the soil or in rocks. Horizon is also the point in the distance at which the land seems to meet the sky.
The fossils were all found in the same horizon within the rocks.

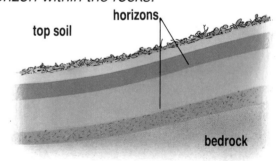

horizons
top soil
bedrock

hornblende   *noun*
Hornblende is a dark green or brown **mineral**. Hornblende is made of **sodium**, **calcium**, **magnesium**, **iron**, and **aluminum**, combined with **silica**.
Hornblende may be found in granite rocks.

hot spot   *noun*
A hot spot is a region in the Earth's **mantle** where molten rocks, or **magma**, rise upward through the **crust**. A **volcano** forms where a hot-spot reaches the surface of the Earth.
There are many hot spots along the Pacific Rim.

hot spring   *noun*
A hot spring is a **spring** in which the water comes out at a high **temperature**. Hot springs are found in those places where there is **volcanic** activity near the surface of the Earth.
Iceland and New Zealand are famous for their hot springs.

humid   *adjective*
Humid describes the **atmosphere** when it contains a large amount of water **vapor**. Warm air holds more water vapor than cold air, so it can be more humid.
The air in a tropical rain forest is very hot and humid.

humidity   *noun*
Humidity is a measure of the level of water **vapor** in the **atmosphere**. When air is completely saturated with water vapor, it reaches its **dew point** and the water **condenses** as droplets.
We began to sweat because the humidity was so high.

humus   *noun*
Humus is the **organic** material in soil. It is made up of the remains of plants and animals. It is a rich source of the **chemicals** needed by growing plants.
Fallen leaves decompose and turn into humus in the soil.

hurricane ► page 72

hydro-   *prefix*
Hydro- is a prefix used to refer to water.
The hydroelectric power station converted the flow of water into electricity.

hydrocarbon   *noun*
A hydrocarbon is a **compound** made of **hydrogen** and **carbon**. Hydrocarbons are the most important chemicals found in **oil** and they are used to make **fuels**.
Methane gas is an example of a hydrocarbon.

hydroelectric power   *noun*
Hydroelectric power is made by turning the **energy** of moving water into electricity. Water from a **reservoir** flows rapidly through a **dam**. This fast-flowing water spins a turbine which generates electricity.
Hydroelectric power is an important source of energy in mountainous areas with a high rainfall.

hydroelectric power station

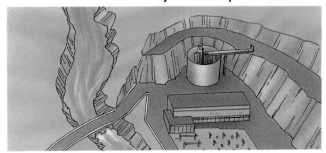

hydrogen   *noun*
Hydrogen is the lightest of all the **elements**. It is a **gas**. Hydrogen is usually found in **compounds**, especially in water and in **hydrocarbons** such as methane.
Water is made up of hydrogen combined with oxygen.

hydrography   *noun*
Hydrography is the making of **maps** or **charts** of the waters of the world.
Hydrography includes surveying rivers, lakes, oceans, and the coast.

hydrology   *noun*
Hydrology is the study of **water** in the **environment**. It involves studying rivers and **oceans**, as well as water in the ground and in the air.
The hydrology of the area was studied carefully before the new buildings were constructed.

71

hurricane *noun*

A hurricane is the strongest kind of **wind**. A hurricane blows in a circular pattern with an area of calm air, called the eye, in its center. The winds of a hurricane are accompanied by heavy **rain** and **thunderstorms**. A hurricane measures force 12 on the **Beaufort Scale**. In Southeast Asia a hurricane is called a typhoon.

The whole village was destroyed when the hurricane passed through.

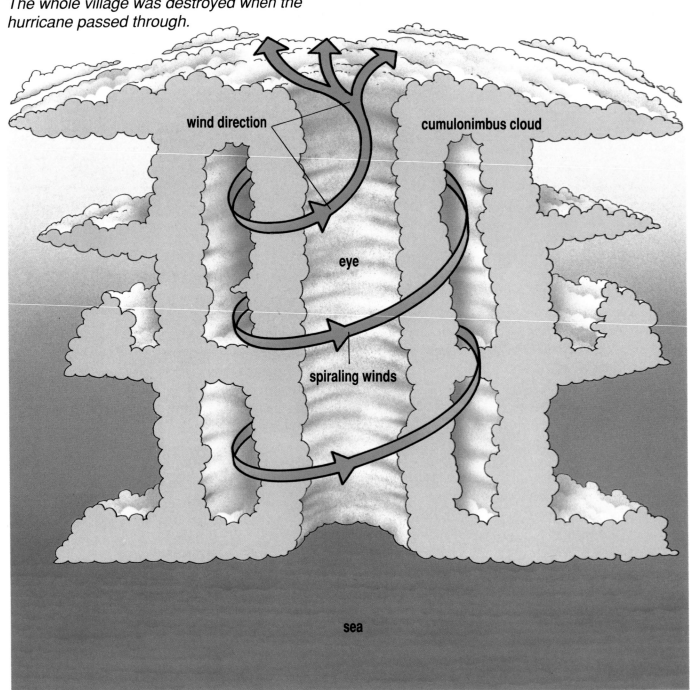

wind direction

cumulonimbus cloud

eye

spiraling winds

sea

hydrolysis *noun*
Hydrolysis is the chemical **weathering** of rocks. Water combines with minerals in the rocks to make **salts** that cannot dissolve. Hydrolysis often takes place in **igneous** rocks that contain **silica**. Hydrolysis usually leads to the formation of **clay**.
The rocks showed clear signs of hydrolysis.

hydrosphere *noun*
The hydrosphere describes all the natural **water** found on the **Earth**. The hydrosphere includes the oceans, rivers, lakes, underground water, and the water **vapor** in the **atmosphere**.
Life on Earth depends on the hydrosphere because all living things need water.

hydroxide *noun*
A hydroxide is a chemical **compound** that contains **hydrogen** and **oxygen**. Water is the hydroxide of hydrogen. Another hydroxide is lye, which is sodium hydroxide.
Sodium hydroxide can be used is a cleaning agent.

hygrometer *noun*
A hygrometer is an instrument used for measuring the **humidity** of the **atmosphere**. In one kind of hygrometer, there are two **thermometers**, one dry and one wet. The difference in **temperature** between the two gives a measure of humidity.
While it was raining, the hygrometer reading was 1.

hygroscope *noun*
A hygroscope records changes in the **humidity** of the **atmosphere**. A strip of seaweed can be used as a simple hygroscope. When the atmosphere is **humid**, the seaweed feels soft and bends easily. When the atmosphere is dry, the seaweed is hard and brittle.
While it was raining, the hygroscope reading remained steady.

ice *noun*
Ice is frozen **water**. Pure water freezes at 0 **degrees** Celsius. Salt water freezes at a lower temperature, so the sea freezes only when it is very cold. When water becomes ice, it swells and takes up more space. Ice is lighter than water, so it floats on the surface of water.
The water turned to ice inside the crack in the rock and made the crack bigger.

ice floating on the water

Ice Age *noun*
An Ice Age is a period when the **climate** is very cold. It can last for many centuries. During an Ice Age, **ice sheets** and **glaciers** cover large areas of the Earth. The most recent Ice Age was about 15,000 years ago.
During the last Ice Age, most of northern Europe was covered by ice.

iceberg   *noun*
An iceberg is a large piece of **ice** floating in the sea. Icebergs break off from **ice sheets** or from **glaciers** and drift on ocean **currents**. Only about one ninth of an iceberg can be seen above the water.
The ocean liner Titanic *hit an iceberg during its first ocean crossing.*

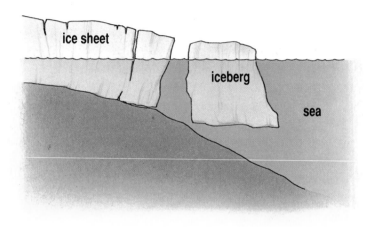

icecap   *noun*
An icecap is a covering of **ice** on an area of land. Some mountains have permanent icecaps. An icecap is larger than a **glacier**, but smaller and thinner than an **ice sheet**. The **South Pole** lies on the Antarctic icecap.
Some of the Earth's oldest rocks are found at the edge of the Greenland icecap.

ice field   *noun*
An ice field is an area of **ice** that is floating in the **sea**. It usually measures more than 6 miles across.
The explorers crossed many ice fields on their way to the North Pole.

ice floe   *noun*
An ice floe is a flat piece of **ice**, adrift in the sea. Ice floes often break away from the edges of **ice fields**. Ice floes are common in the cold seas of the **Arctic** and **Antarctica**. They vary in size from several feet to two thousand feet or so wide.
The sea around the ice field was dotted with ice floes.

ice sheet   *noun*
An ice sheet is a large, thick layer of **ice** covering an area of land. There are many ice sheets in Greenland and in **Antarctica**. Ice sheets are bigger and thicker than **icecaps**.
The flat ice sheet stretched into the distance.

icicle   *noun*
An icicle is a hanging spike of clear **ice** formed from dripping water. As the water trickles down the icicle, it freezes. This gradually makes the icicle thicker and longer. Icicles often hang from the roofs of houses in very cold weather.
In the morning, there was an icicle on the leaky water faucet.

igneous   *adjective*
Igneous describes a kind of **rock** or **stone**. Igneous rocks are formed from molten material inside the Earth. Some igneous rocks form underground. Others form from the **lava** thrown out by an erupting **volcano**. The other kinds of rock are **sedimentary** and **metamorphic**.
The slopes of the volcano were made of igneous rocks.

illite   *noun*
Illite is a common **clay** mineral found in some soils and on the **seabed**. The name comes from the state of Illinois, where it is very common. Some plants cannot grow well in soil that contains illite since the illite absorbs the **potassium** and ammonium that the plants need.
The geologist found that the soil contained large amounts of illite.

impermeable   *adjective*
Impermeable describes something through which **water** cannot pass. The opposite of impermeable is **permeable**.
The water collected in the hollow above a layer of impermeable clay.

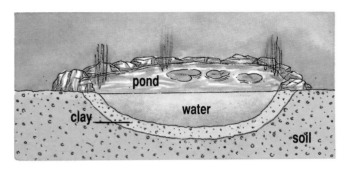

impervious   *adjective*
Impervious describes materials through that water cannot pass. Rocks that do not have gaps or cracks may be impervious. The opposite of impervious is **pervious**.
The stone building was impervious to water.

impurity   *noun*
An impurity is a small amount of another substance found in a pure substance. Sometimes, an impurity can change the pure substance. Pure **corundum** is a colorless **crystal**. But crystals of corundum that contain **chromium** are red **rubies.**
The chemist filtered out the impurity to obtain pure water.

inert   *adjective*
Inert describes **gases** that do not react easily with other **chemicals**. Inert gases include **helium**, **neon**, **argon**, **krypton**, and **radon**.
The fluorescent light bulb contained inert gases.

infertile   *adjective*
Infertile describes something that cannot support growth. Plants cannot grow in infertile **soil**. Infertile also describes an animal or plant that cannot produce young or seeds.
The crops did not grow because the ground was infertile.

inland   *adjective*
Inland describes land that is away from the sea, in the middle of a country or region.
The inland road took them away from the coast toward the mountains.

inlet   *noun*
An inlet is a short, narrow opening that runs **inland** from a large stretch of water. **Lakes** and **coasts** often have many inlets.
The canoe moved slowly between the banks of the narrow inlet.

inner core   *noun*
The inner core is the central part of the **Earth**. It lies about 2,700 miles deep and is surrounded by the **outer core**. The inner core is solid and is mainly made of **iron** and **nickel**. The inner core of the Earth is a **magnet**. Scientists think the temperature is about 2,700 degrees Celsius. (See illustration page 43.)
The diagram showed the inner core as a ball of molten metal at the center of the Earth.

inorganic   *adjective*
Inorganic is used to describe substances that do not contain any of the **organic** chemicals that make up living things. The rocks of the Earth's **crust** are inorganic. The opposite of inorganic is organic.
There were layers of coal among the inorganic rocks.

intensity   *noun*
Intensity is used to describe the force of a natural event, such as an **earthquake**. The intensity of an earthquake is measured on the **Richter Scale**. Intensity is also used to describe **rainfall**, which can be heavy, moderate, or light in intensity.
The intensity of the earthquake was so great that the city was completely destroyed.

inter-   *prefix*
Inter- is a prefix meaning between or among.
An international arrangement allows scientists from many countries to work in Antarctica.

interglacial period   *noun*
An interglacial period is the time between two periods of **glaciation**. During an interglacial period, the **temperature** on the Earth is higher than during glaciation, **glaciers** melt, and the **sea level** may rise.
The ice sheets melted in the warmer temperatures of the interglacial period.

International Date Line   *noun*
The International Date Line is an imaginary line drawn through the Pacific Ocean roughly along the 180 degrees **meridian**. It is where each new calendar day begins. When it is Monday to the west of the line, it will be Sunday to the east of the line.
Travelers who cross the International Date Line can "lose" or "gain" a whole day.

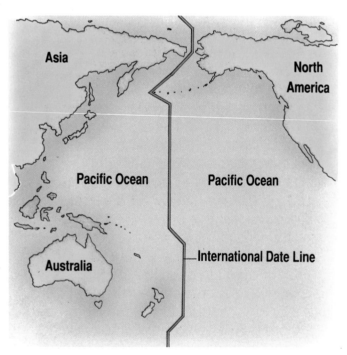

intertidal zone   *noun*
The intertidal zone is an area of the **seashore** covered by water at high **tide** and dry at low tide. It is part of the **littoral zone**. Some animals and plants are found only in the intertidal zone.
In many parts of the world, the sea covers the intertidal zone twice each day.

intrusion   *noun*
An intrusion is a piece of **igneous** rock found inside another rock. An intrusion squeezes into other rocks when it is **molten**. **Gems** and **minerals** can be found in intrusions.
The geologist discovered the intrusion in the rock face.

inversion   *noun*
An inversion describes a change that is exactly the opposite to what is normally experienced. A **temperature** inversion can happen when the air becomes warmer with **altitude**, rather than colder. It can also happen in some lakes when the deep water is warmer than the water at the surface.
The temperature inversion resulted in frost covering the bottom of the valley.

iodine   *noun*
Iodine is an **element** composed of grayish-black **crystals**. All living things need iodine to grow. Some iodine **compounds** can be used to prevent infection.
Iodine can be used as a disinfectant.

ionosphere   *noun*
The ionosphere is part of the Earth's **atmosphere**. The ionosphere lies above the **stratopause**, starting about 48 miles above the surface of the Earth. (See page 10.)
Many magnetic storms take place in the ionosphere.

iron   *noun*
Iron is an **element**. It is a dark gray **metal** that reacts with damp air to form rust, which is a reddish-brown color. Iron is a very common **element** in the Earth's **crust**.
The iron nail became rusty quickly in the moist air.

iron ore   *noun*
Iron ore is a **mineral** that contains **iron**. There are several different kinds of iron ore, the main ones being **hematite**, **magnetite**, **limonite**, and **pyrite**.
The factory produced iron from iron ore.

irrigation *noun*

Irrigation is the method of taking **water** to dry land where there is not enough rainfall for crops to grow. The water is carried in **canals** and ditches from a river or other source of water and spread by sprinklers or pipes.
Crops can be grown in desert areas where irrigation provides water.

irrigate *verb*

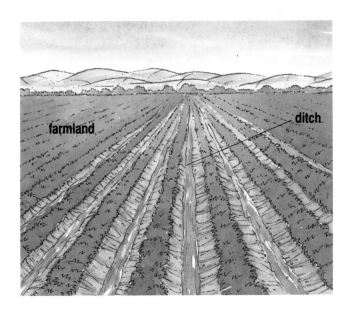

island *noun*

An island is an area of **land** entirely surrounded by **water**. An island can be only a few feet across or several thousand miles wide. The largest island on Earth is the **continent** of Australia.
We sailed around the entire island in a day.

iso- *prefix*

Iso- is a prefix meaning equal.
The isotherm lines on the map showed which places had equal temperature.

isobar *noun*

An isobar is a line drawn on a **weather map** to join points of equal **pressure**. If the isobars on a weather map are close together, the winds are strong.
The distance between the isobars on the map indicated calm weather.

isobath *noun*

An isobath is a line drawn on a **chart** of the sea or a lake joining points on the **seabed** or on the bottom of a lake that are at the same depth from the surface.
Sailors relay on isobaths to steer clear of shallow water.

isotherm *noun*

An isotherm is a line on a **weather map** that joins places on the Earth's surface where the **temperature** is the same.
The isotherm showed that the temperature that day was the same in Denver as it was in New York.

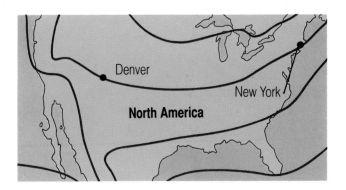

isthmus *noun*

An isthmus is a long, narrow strip of land that joins together two large **land masses**. There is sea on either side of an isthmus. *The Isthmus of Panama joins North America and South America and lies between the Atlantic and Pacific oceans.*

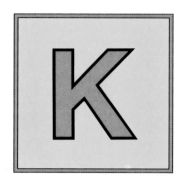

jade *noun*

Jade is a hard, semiprecious stone often used as a **gem**. It can be many colors, including green, white, brown, or orange. Jade is made up of jadeite or **nephrite**. Nephrite is the more common of the two **minerals** and is mostly found in New Zealand.
Jade can be carved into delicate shapes because it is so tough.

jet *noun*

Jet is a hard form of **coal**. When it is cut and polished, it is very shiny and looks like black glass. It is used to make jewelry and ornaments.
The earrings made from bright, black stones of jet sparkled in the light.

jet stream *noun*

The jet stream is a narrow band of fast-moving **winds** that is found at high **altitudes**. There are several jet streams which change position and speed at different times of the year.
The plane traveling in the jet stream and arrived ahead of schedule.

Jurassic *adjective*

Jurassic describes the **period** in **geological time** from about 213 million years ago to about 144 million years ago. The biggest **dinosaurs** lived in the Jurassic Period. (See chart page 64.)
Some of today's species of ferns also grew during the Jurassic Period.

kaolin ► China clay

Karroo *noun*

The Karroo is an area of southern Africa where the **climate** is very dry. The plants growing there have adapted to living in dry conditions.
Farmers must use irrigation to grow crops in the Karroo.

karst *noun*

Karst is the name for a type of **landscape** where **limestone** rocks are found near the surface. Karst regions have many underground streams and rivers, where the water has worn passages through the limestone.
Karst areas are well known for their deep caves.

key *noun*

A key, or cay, is a small, flat **island**. It is made of **sand** that has built up in shallow water. The surface of the island lies only just above the water at high **tide**. Keys are found in **coral reefs** and in the United States in Florida.
The sailors spotted the keys on the horizon.

khamsin *noun*

The khamsin is a very hot, dry, dusty **wind** blowing from the south, across the Sahara in north Africa. The khamsin usually blows from April to June.
The khamsin makes travel in the Sahara especially difficult.

kieselguhr *noun*

Kieselguhr is a soft and fine-grained rock. It is made up of the shells of tiny plants that lived in water. Kieselguhr has many uses in industry.
The impurities in the water were removed as it filtered through the bed of kieselguhr.

knoll *noun*

A knoll is a small, rounded **hill**.
The ball rolled down the slope of the grassy knoll.

krypton *noun*

The **element** krypton is a **gas** that is found in small amounts in the **atmosphere**. Krypton is an **inert** gas and forms very few **compounds** with other elements.
The fluorescent lamp was filled with a mixture of gases, including krypton.

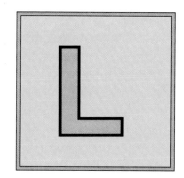

labradorite *noun*

Labradorite is a **mineral**. It is a grayish-white kind of **feldspar**. In the light, labradorite may show blue, green, and red colors, especially where it is cut. It was first found at Labrador in Canada.
The building was decorated with attractive labradorite stones.

lagoon *noun*

A lagoon is a shallow pool of salt water near the **coast**. A lagoon is usually cut off from the sea by a ridge of sand or **shingle**. In an **atoll**, the central lagoon is surrounded by a **coral reef**.
We swam safely in the lagoon because the water was so shallow.

lake *noun*

A lake is a large piece of water that is completely surrounded by land. Most lakes contain fresh water, but there are also some salt-water lakes. Some lakes have rivers flowing through them.
The rowboats were out on the lake throughout the summer.

land *noun*

Land is the solid part of the surface of the **Earth**. The Earth's surface is covered by land, sea, and fresh water.
A surveyor mapped the contours of the land.

land mass *noun*

A land mass is a large piece of **land**, such as a **continent**.
The land mass around the South Pole is called Antarctica.

landscape *noun*
Landscape is a word that describes an area of country. Landscape includes the natural scenery, buildings, and roads.
The landscape was dotted with trees.

landslide *noun*
A landslide is a fall of rocks and earth down a steep **slope**. A landslide can happen after heavy rain has loosened the surface of the soil. **Earthquakes** and **mining** can also cause landslides.
The whole village was buried under the landslide.

lapilli *noun*
Lapilli are small pieces of volcanic material only a fraction of an inch across. They are thrown out of a **volcano** when it **erupts**.
The lapilli fell to the ground some distance from the volcano.

lapis lazuli *noun*
Lapis lazuli is a deep blue, semiprecious stone. It is made mostly of the blue **mineral** lazurite and also contains the mineral **calcite**.
A deep blue paint can be made from powdered lapis lazuli.

large-scale *adjective*
Large-scale is a term used when something is shown in great detail. A large-scale **map** covers all the features of a small area. A large-scale diagram is drawn large enough to show a very detailed view of the subject.
Builders must use large-scale maps to plan their projects carefully.

laterite *noun*
Laterite is a red and sandy **soil** that contains **iron** and **aluminum** oxides. It is formed by the **weathering** of certain kinds of rock, mostly **volcanic** rock, in the **tropics**. Laterite is mostly formed from **volcanic** rocks.
The red road was made from crushed laterite.

latitude *noun*
Latitude is an imaginary line drawn horizontally around the Earth, parallel to the **Equator** used to measure distance from the Equator. There are 90 **degrees** of latitude on each side of the Equator. Places of equal distance from the Equator lie on the same **parallel** of latitude. On **maps**, latitude measures the vertical position, and **longitude** the horizontal distance of a point.
The Equator is 0 degrees latitude and the poles are 90 degrees latitude.

Laurasia *noun*
Laurasia is the name of a large **continent** that some scientists think formed when the **supercontinent** of **Pangaea** split about 215 million years ago, during the **Mesozoic** Era. Laurasia may have gradually split further, to create North America, Greenland, Europe, and Asia. (See illustration page 108.)
This is a map of Laurasia.

lava *noun*
Lava is the **molten** rock that comes out of a **volcano** when it **erupts** or from cracks in the Earth. Lava cools to form **igneous** rock.
Red-hot lava flowing down the slopes of the volcano is a spectacular sight.

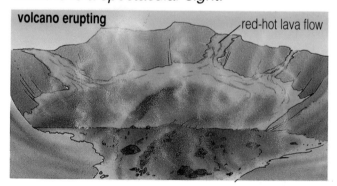

volcano erupting red-hot lava flow

layer *noun*
Layer is a thickness of rock. Each **stratum** in **sedimentary** rock consists of a number of layers.
The geologists found many fossils in the same layer of the rock.

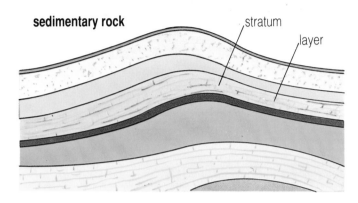

sedimentary rock
stratum
layer

leach *verb*
The draining effects of water as it moves down into the soil. The water removes **salts** from the upper layers of the soil and carries them farther down into the ground. When a soil is leached, the top layers become less **fertile**, and leaching can cause **acid soil**. However, some farmers leach ground to wash away harmful salts.
The heavy rains leached the nutrients from the soil.

lead *noun*
The **element** lead is a very heavy, dark gray **metal**. There are several lead **ores**, including the most common, **galena**. Lead can be used as a building material, in **alloys** with other metals, and in many other ways.
Paints made with lead can be hazardous.

levee *noun*
A levee is a raised **bank** beside a **river**. The levee is higher than the land beyond the river. Levees form when rivers **flood** and the **sediment** from the water is deposited on the edge of the river **channel**. Levees can be built along the sides of a river to stop it from flooding the land.
By walking along the levee, they could see over the river and the fields.

level *noun*
A level is an instrument for measuring height used by map-makers and surveyors. A level shows how high one point is above another.
The surveyor used his level to gauge the height of the hill.

lightning *noun*
Lightning is an electric spark from a **cloud** in a **thunderstorm**. Lightning can be seen as flashes, as balls, or as sheets of light. It is followed by **thunder**.
The lightning lit up the night sky dramatically.

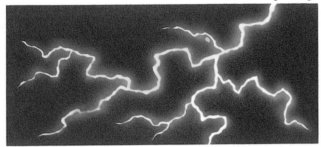

forked lightning

lignite *noun*
Lignite, or brown coal, is a form of **coal** and a kind of **fossil fuel**. It burns with a very smoky flame. It contains about 65 percent **carbon**. Lignite has more carbon in it than **peat**, but less than **anthracite**.
The power station burned lignite to make electricity.

lime *noun*
Lime is a solid, white **compound**. It is also the name used for **salts** of **calcium**. The two forms of lime are quicklime and slaked lime. Quicklime is an **oxide** of calcium and is used as a **fertilizer**. When water is added, quicklime becomes calcium hydroxide or slaked lime, which is used in cements.
The farmer used lime to nourish his crops.

limestone *noun*
Limestone is a kind of **sedimentary** rock. It is often used as a building **stone** because it is easy to cut. Limestone is used to make **lime**. Many plants grow well on limestone soils.
The limestone cliffs shone white in the sun.

limonite *noun*
The **mineral** limonite is a yellow-brown kind of **iron ore**. Very pure iron can be extracted from limonite.
The surveyors found lumps of limonite in the soil.

lithium *noun*
The **element** lithium is a soft, silvery **metal**. Pure lithium is very rare because it joins with other elements so easily. Lithium is used in batteries, for **alloys**, and in medicine.
The lithium batteries are especially long-lasting.

lithosphere *noun*
The lithosphere is the Earth's **crust** and the top of the **mantle**, including the **tectonic plates**. The lithosphere is one part of the outer area of the Earth. The other parts are the **atmosphere** and the **hydrosphere**.
The Earth's rocks and minerals form part of the lithosphere.

littoral zone *noun*
The littoral zone is the area of water and land at the edge of the **seashore** and of lakes. The littoral zone includes the **intertidal** zone and slightly deeper water.
They picked up the shells in the littoral zone.

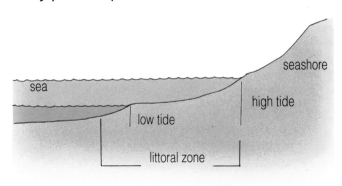

loam *noun*
Loam is a kind of **soil** that is a mixture of **sand**, **silt**, and small amounts of **clay**. Loams are very **fertile** soils.
The farmer grew a good vegetable crop in the deep loam.

lode *noun*
A lode is a **vein** of **minerals** that runs through rock. The lode may be mined, if the mineral is valuable.
The mining engineers found gold deposits in the lode.

lodestone *noun*
Lodestone is a kind of **iron ore** made of **magnetite** that works as a **magnet**. Pieces of lodestone were used as an early form of **compass**. Some of the most powerful lodestones are found in Russia and South Africa.
Lodestones were used by early travelers to find direction.

loess *noun*
Loess is a kind of **soil** that is yellow-colored, light, and rich in **lime**. Loess soils are very **fertile**. Loess can be used to make bricks. Large areas of loess are found in central Europe, the United States, and in China.
The farmer planted his crops in the deep loess.

longitude *noun*
Longitude is an imaginary line drawn vertically around the Earth from the **North Pole** to the **South Pole**. Longitude is a measurement used for distance eastward or westward. All longitudes are measured in **degrees** from the **Greenwich meridian**, which is 0 degrees longitude. On **maps**, longitude measures the horizontal position of a point. The vertical position is measured by **latitude**.
There are 360 degrees of longitude around the Earth.

low pressure *noun*
Low pressure is an area of the **atmosphere** where **atmospheric pressure** is low. During a period of low pressure, or **depression**, the weather is often wet.
The low pressure brought windy and cold weather.

lowlands   *noun*
Lowlands are land that is flat or gently rolling, and that is lower than the land around it. Higher ground with **mountains** is called highlands.
The farmer brought the sheep down to the lowlands for the winter.

luster   *noun*
Luster is the shine on the surface of a **mineral**. Different kinds of stones and minerals have different lusters.
Some gems are prized for their luster.
lustrous   *adjective*

magma   *noun*
Magma is **molten** rock containing **gases**, that is formed in the Earth's **mantle**. Magma sometimes comes to the surface as **lava** when volcanoes **erupt**, or through cracks in the Earth. When magma cools, it forms **igneous** rocks and **stones**.
After the eruption, the magma cooled on the sides of the volcano.

magnesium   *noun*
The **element** magnesium is a silvery-gray **metal**. Magnesium is found in many **minerals** and also in sea water. It burns with a very bright flame.
The crew sent up magnesium flares from the boat to show the rescuers their position.

magnet   *noun*
A magnet is an object, usually made of **metal**, that attracts other metal objects. Magnets have two **magnetic poles**. The **core** of the **Earth** acts as a giant magnet.
A compass needle is a type of magnet.
magnetic   *adjective*

magnetic field   *noun*
A magnetic field is the area affected by a **magnet**. The **Earth** is surrounded by a magnetic field.
The compass worked in the magnetic field.

magnetic north   *noun*
Magnetic north is the position of the **magnetic pole** at the northern point of the **Earth**. It is in Canada, near the geographic **North Pole**.
The explorer walked toward magnetic north.

83

magnetic pole *noun*

A magnetic pole is an area of strong magnetic force at the end of a **magnet**. The **Earth** is a magnet, and has a magnetic pole at either end of its magnetic field. The **magnetic north** pole and the **magnetic south** pole are some distance away from the geographical **North Pole** and **South Pole**. *The exact positions of the magnetic poles change slowly over time.*

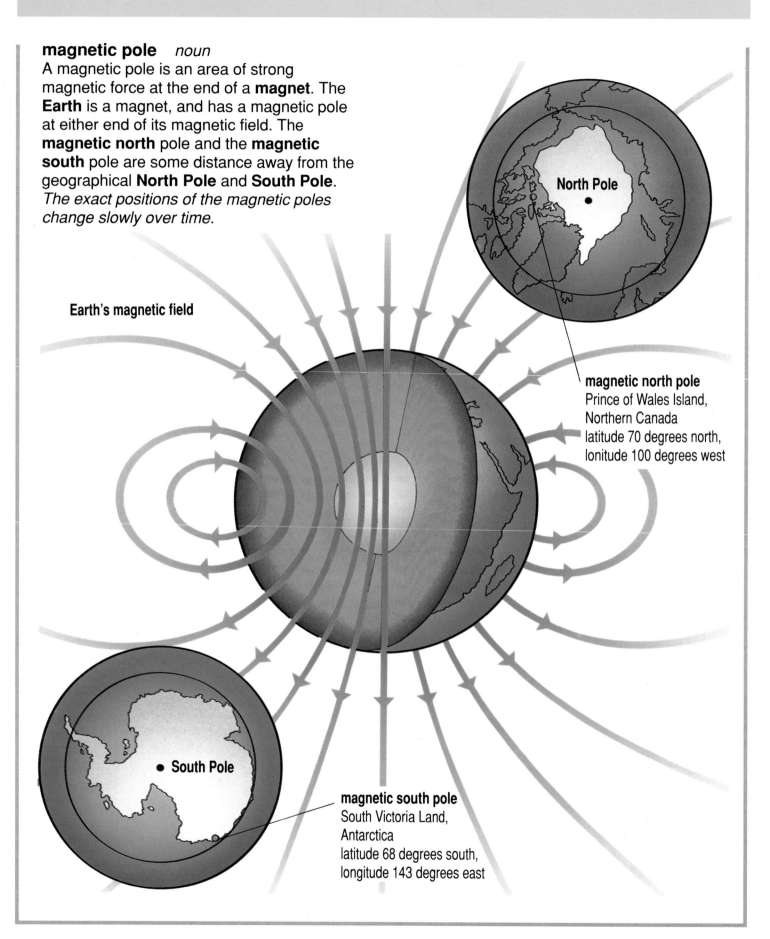

Earth's magnetic field

North Pole

magnetic north pole
Prince of Wales Island,
Northern Canada
latitude 70 degrees north,
lonitude 100 degrees west

• South Pole

magnetic south pole
South Victoria Land,
Antarctica
latitude 68 degrees south,
longitude 143 degrees east

magnetic pole ▶ page 84

magnetic south   *noun*
Magnetic south is the position of the
magnetic pole at the southern point of the
Earth. The magnetic south is in the
continent of **Antarctica**, near the
geographic **South Pole**.
The magnetic needle swung toward
magnetic south.

magnetic storm   *noun*
A magnetic storm is a disturbance in the
Earth's **magnetic field**. It is caused by
changes in the activity of the Sun. Magnetic
storms can interfere with radio waves and
satellites.
Radio reception was cut off during the
magnetic storm.

magnetite   *noun*
Magnetite, or **lodestone**, is a kind of black
iron ore containing **crystals** of iron **oxide**.
Magnetite is strongly **magnetic**.
The rock contained pieces of magnetite.

magnitude   *noun*
Magnitude describes the force of an
earthquake. The magnitude of an earthquake
is measured on the **Richter Scale**.
Although the earthquake had a low
magnitude, it still caused a lot of damage.

malachite   *noun*
Malachite is a bright green **mineral** made of
copper **carbonate**. Copper can be extracted
from malachite. Malachite is also used as a
semiprecious stone.
Polished malachite is often used to make
necklaces and earrings.

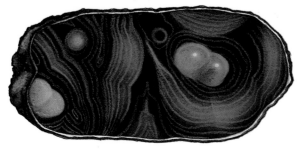

manganese   *noun*
Manganese is an **element**. It is a hard **metal**
that is found as manganese **oxide** in some
rocks. Manganese also occurs in **clay** and in
the **mud** on the ocean floor. All plants and
animals need a small amount of manganese
to grow properly.
There was not enough manganese in the soil
to grow food crops.

mantle   *noun*
The mantle is the part of the **Earth** that lies
between the **crust** and the **core**. The mantle
is mostly solid **rock**, but some of the rocks
are **molten**. The movements of molten rock
in the mantle cause **continental drift** and
sea-floor spreading.
Earth scientists are still discovering new facts
about the activity in the Earth's mantle.

map ▶ page 86

marble   *noun*
Marble is **limestone** that has changed to
metamorphic rock. It is very hard, and can
be cut and polished. Marble is used as a
building **stone**. Pure marble is white, but if it
contains **impurities**, it has mottled or veined
patterns.
Polished marble is an elegant, but
expensive, building material.

marine   *adjective*
Marine refers to the sea. Marine **abrasion**
occurs along **coasts** when the waves push
sand and **shingle** backward and forward.
Marine biologists study all the plants and
creatures that live in the sea.

maritime   *adjective*
Maritime describes something that is near
the sea or that is affected by the sea. A
maritime climate is **temperate**, and has mild
weather all year. The temperatures change
little from **winter** to **summer**, and there is no
dry season.
The maritime provinces of Canada are those
close to the Atlantic Ocean.

map *noun*

A map is a **scale** drawing of a country or a region. For example, one inch of distance on the map may stand for one mile of distance on the surface of the Earth. Maps show features of the landscape, such as hills, roads, and rivers, in diagrammatic form. *The relief map and the contour map show different views of the same place.*

In a **contour map**, all the points joined by a contour line are at the same height above sea level.

A **relief map** illustrates features of a landscape including geological formations and bodies of water.

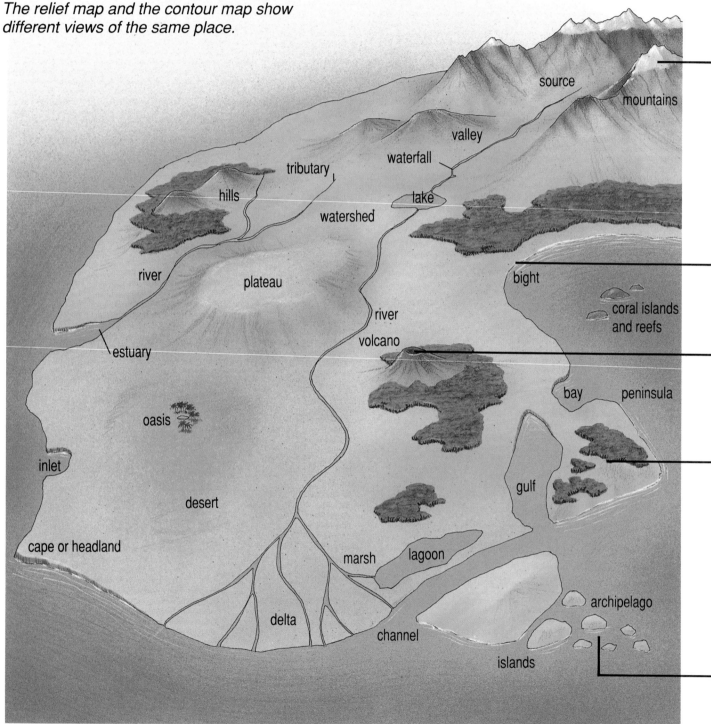

source

mountains

valley

waterfall

tributary

hills

lake

watershed

river

plateau

bight

coral islands and reefs

river

volcano

estuary

bay   peninsula

oasis

inlet

gulf

desert

cape or headland

marsh   lagoon

delta

archipelago

channel

islands

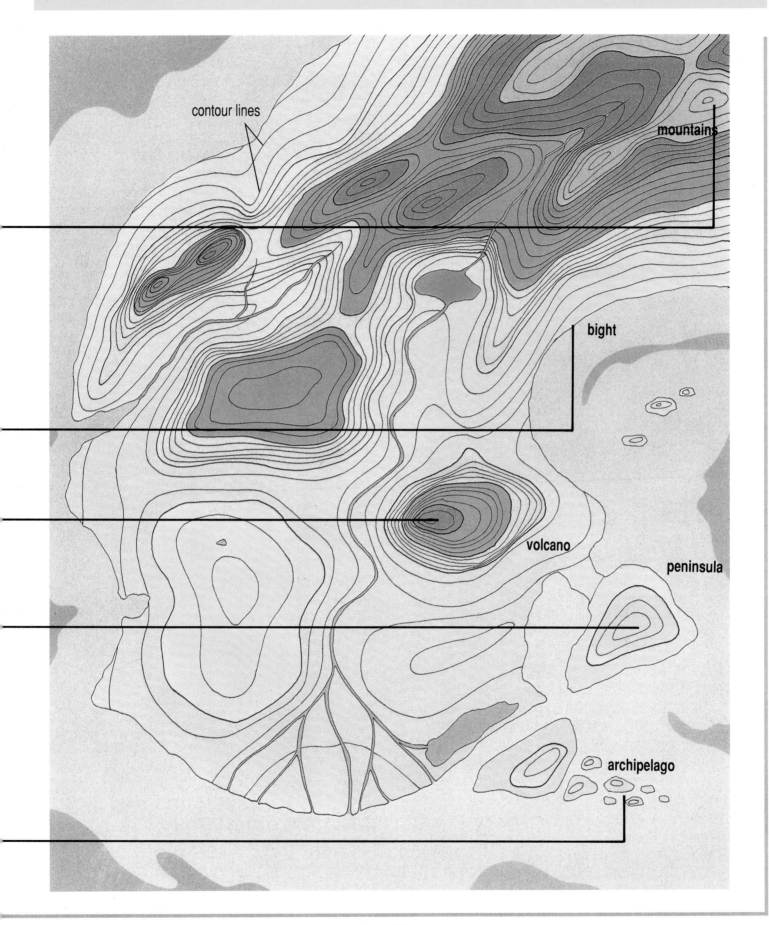

contour lines

mountains

bight

volcano

peninsula

archipelago

marsh   *noun*

A marsh is an area of low, wet ground. In a marsh, the **drainage** is poor and the water often floods over the surface. Marshes can form at **estuaries** when the land becomes flooded with salt water.

Certain kinds of animals have adapted to life in a marsh.

wet ground

massif   *noun*

A massif is a large **mountain** or group of mountains. A massif stands out clearly from the surrounding **lowlands**.

The massif towered over the landscape and could be seen from far away.

matter   *noun*

Matter is anything that has mass (weight) and takes up space. The three kinds of matter are solids, liquids, and **gases**.

Many scientists think that the Earth is made from matter which came from the Sun.

meander   *noun*

A meander is a snake-like bend in a **river**. Lowland rivers often have many meanders along their length. Sometimes, a meander is cut off from the rest of the river and becomes an **oxbow lake**.

The river flowed in a series of meanders.

Mercalli Scale ► page 89

Mercator projection   *noun*

The Mercator projection, a cylindrical **projection**, is a way of drawing a **map** of the **Earth**. On the Mercator projection, all the lines of **latitude** and **longitude** are drawn parallel to each other. On this projection, the countries near the **poles** seem larger than they really are. (See illustration page 114.)

Maps drawn with a Mercator projection are often used for navigation.

mercury   *noun*

Mercury is an **element**. A silvery **metal**, mercury is the only metal which is liquid at room **temperature**. Mercury is used in **thermometers** and in **alloys**.

As the temperature rose, the mercury moved quickly up the thermometer.

meridian   *noun*

A meridian is an imaginary line drawn vertically around the **Earth**. The meridians run from the **North Pole** to the **South Pole** and across the **Equator** at a right angle. Meridians are measurements of **longitude**, numbered from 0 to 180 degrees to the east and to the west of the **Greenwich meridian**. The Greenwich meridian is 0 degrees longitude.

The meridian at 60 degrees west passes through the center of South America.

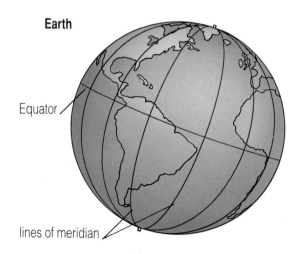

Earth

Equator

lines of meridian

Mercalli Scale *noun*

The Mercalli Scale is an older scale used for measuring the amount of damage caused by an **earthquake**. It has 12 grades. The strength of an earthquake is now usually measured on the **Richter Scale**.

The violent earthquake measured 10 on the Mercalli Scale.

1
tremors can be recorded by scientific instruments, but not felt by people

2
tremors felt by a few people

3
tremors felt indoors, stationary cars may rock

4
cars rock, windows and dishes rattle, pictures swing

5
sleepers roused, plaster falls, windows and dishes break

6
furniture moves, chimneys damaged, small bells ring

7
badly-built structures damaged, large bells ring, waves formed on ponds

8
more buildings damaged, furniture overturned

9
most buildings damaged, some destroyed, underground pipes break

10
most buildings and some bridges destroyed, rails slightly bent, landslides

11
few buildings survive, rails badly bent, underground pipes all damaged

12
total destruction

mesa *noun*

A mesa is an isolated **hill** with a flat top, like a table with a **cliff** or steep slope at the edges. Mesas are most often found in dry **climates**.
The explorers found caves at the base of the mesa.

Mesozoic *adjective*

Mesozoic is one of the three major **eras** in **geological time**. The Mesozoic Era lasted from about 248 million years ago until about 65 million years ago. Some scientists think that during this time the **continents** that we know today separated from **Laurasia** and **Gondwanaland**. The Mesozoic Era is divided into the **Triassic**, the **Jurassic**, and the **Cretaceous** periods. (See chart page 64.)
Many reptiles lived on the Earth during the Mesozoic Era.

metal *noun*

A metal is a kind of **element**. Unlike other elements, metals can conduct **heat** and electricity. Metals combine with **oxygen** to make **compounds** called **oxides**. About three-quarters of all elements are metals.
Gold, tin, and aluminum are all metals.

metallurgist *noun*

A metallurgist is a scientist who studies **metallurgy**.
The metallurgist tested the iron ore for purity in the laboratory.

metallurgy *noun*

Metallurgy is the study of metals and their **alloys**. In metallurgy, scientists examine the physical and **chemical** properties of metals.
Metallurgy is an important part of the automobile industry.

metamorphic *adjective*

Metamorphic describes one of the three main kinds of **rock** or **stone**. The structure of metamorphic rocks has been changed by heat, high **pressure**, or water. Metamorphic rocks are usually harder than the rocks from which they were formed. The other kinds of rock are **igneous** and **sedimentary** rock.
Schist, gneiss, slate, and marble are all metamorphic rocks.

meteorite *noun*

A meteorite is a piece of solid **mineral** from space that lands on the surface of the **Earth**. Meteorites contain large amounts of **silica**, **nickel**, and **iron**.
The impact of the meteorite left a deep crater in the field.

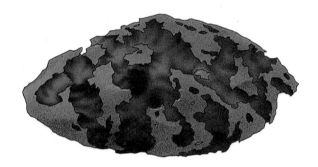

meteorograph *noun*

A meteorograph is an instrument used by **meteorologists** to record information about the Earth's **atmosphere**. It is attached to a balloon and floats in the **stratosphere**.
A meteorograph can ascend higher in the atmosphere than an airplane.

meteorologist *noun*

A meteorologist is a scientist who studies **meteorology**. Meteorologists can predict changes in the **weather** and make **weather forecasts**.
The meteorologist predicted that it would rain.

meteorology *noun*

Meteorology is the study of the **atmosphere** and **weather** of the **Earth**.
Many complex scientific instruments are used in meteorology.

methane *noun*
Methane is a **gas** made of **carbon** and **hydrogen**. It is formed when **organic** substances decompose and is sometimes called marsh gas. **Natural gas** is mostly made up of methane.
The methane burned with a clear flame.

mica *noun*
Mica is a kind of **mineral** that contains **potassium**, **aluminum**, and **silicon**. Mica is smooth and breaks easily into sheets.
The rock contained flaky deposits of mica.

mid-oceanic ridge *noun*
A mid-oceanic ridge is a long range of **mountains** on the **ocean** floor. **Sea-floor spreading** creates new **oceanic crust** at the mid-ocean ridges. There are mid-oceanic ridges in the north and south Atlantic oceans, and in the Indian Ocean.
The sea was not as deep over the mid-oceanic ridge.

millibar ► bar

mine *noun*
A mine is a deep pit in the ground. Mines are dug to extract **coal**, **metals**, and **minerals** such as diamonds. Some of the world's mines are very deep.
The mine had many underground tunnels that were connected together.

mineral ► page 92

mineral salt ► salt

mineral water *noun*
Mineral water is water that comes from **springs** in the **Earth**. Different kinds of mineral water contain different mineral **salts**. A few types of mineral water are fizzy because they contain **carbon dioxide**. Mineral waters are sometimes used for treating illnesses such as rheumatism and arthritis, or for general health.
Many people prefer mineral water.

mineralogist *noun*
A mineralogist is a scientist who studies **mineralogy**. Mining companies often ask mineralogists to test new mining sites.
The mineralogist tested the area for metal deposits.

mineralogy *noun*
Mineralogy deals with the physical and **chemical** properties of **minerals**, such as their color, **crystal** shape, hardness, and **luster**.
Many amateur rock collectors have studied the basics of mineralogy.

mining *noun*
Mining is the process of taking **metals**, valuable stones, and **minerals** from the Earth. Most mining is done with large machines, such as drills and diggers.
Mining can take place on the Earth's surface or under the ground.

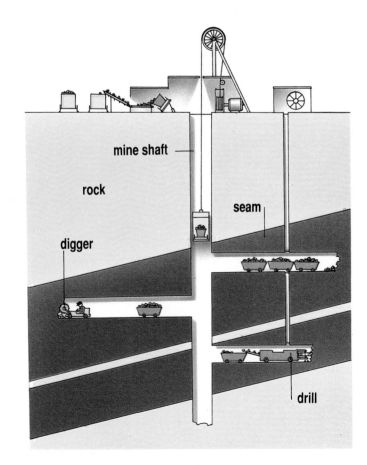

mineral *noun*

A mineral is an inorganic **chemical** found in the **earth** or in **rocks**. Most minerals are made up of **crystals**, and many of them are hard. There are more than 200 known minerals.

Minerals were extracted from the hillside mine.

claystone

quartz

granite

slate

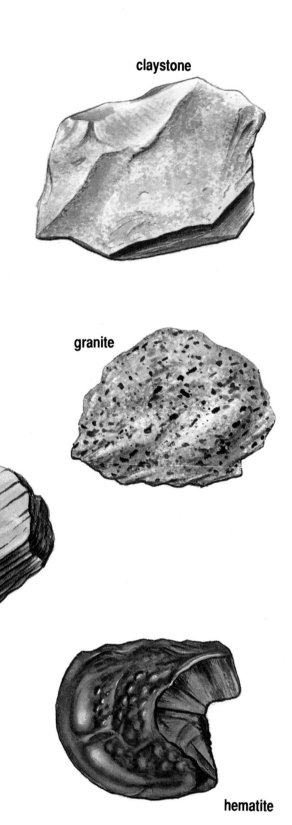

feldspar

hematite

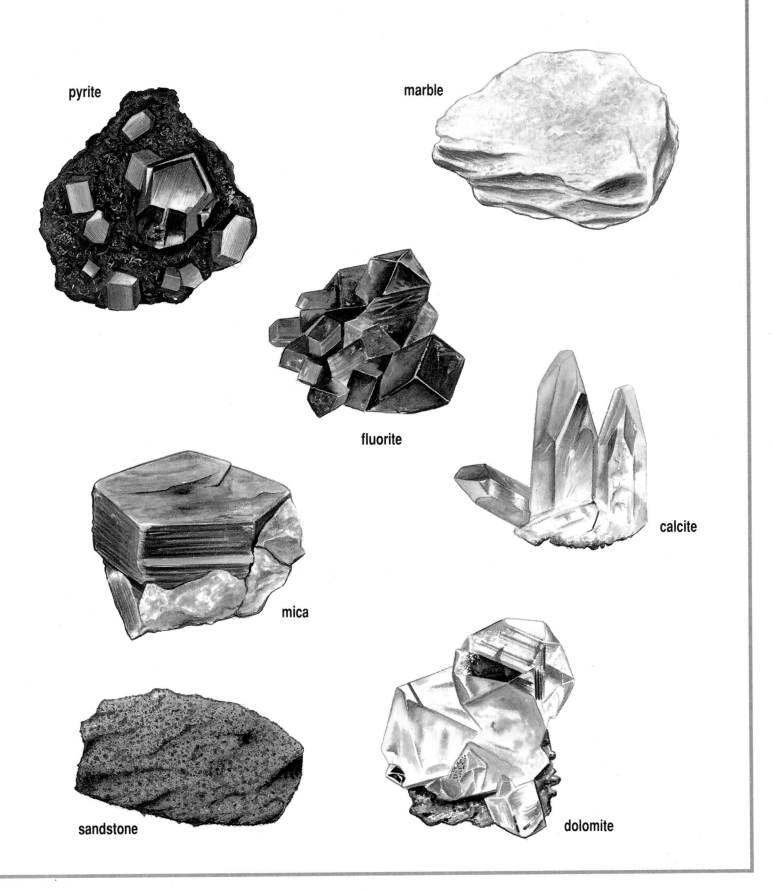

pyrite

marble

fluorite

calcite

mica

sandstone

dolomite

93

Miocene   *adjective*
Miocene describes an **epoch** in **geological time**. The Miocene Epoch occurred in the **Tertiary** Period and lasted from about 24.6 million years ago to about 5.1 million years ago. Some scientists think that a human-like creature first appeared during the Miocene Epoch. (see chart page 64.)
The ancestors of many of today's species of mammals lived on the Earth during the Miocene Epoch.

Mississippian   *adjective*
Mississippian describes a subperiod in **geological time**. It is the term used in North America for the most recent part of the **Carboniferous** Period from about 360 million years ago to about 320 million years ago. (See chart page 64.)
There was much volcanic activity during the Mississippian sub-period.

mist   *noun*
Mist is tiny drops of **water** suspended in the air. When **clouds** form at ground level, it is called mist. It is thicker than **haze**, but it is not as thick as **fog**.
We could not see the mountains through the mist.

mistral   *noun*
The mistral is the name of a strong, cool, dry **wind** that blows from the Alps across southern France toward the Mediterranean Sea. The mistral can blow at up to 35 miles per hour, usually in **winter**.
The grape harvest was damaged by the cold mistral.

moisture   *noun*
Moisture is the amount of water **vapor** in the air or on a surface. Dry air contains very little moisture. A high moisture level can lead to the formation of **clouds**. The amount of water vapor in the air is also called **humidity**.
The moisture in the air made us feel uncomfortable.
moist   *adjective*

molten   *adjective*
Molten describes solids that have been heated above their melting point and have turned to liquid. Molten rock is called **magma**. The **outer core**, deep inside the **Earth**, is also molten.
The molten rock came out of the erupting volcano as lava.

molten lava   **erupting volcano**

molybdenum   *noun*
Molybdenum is an **element**. Pure molybdenum is a gray, silvery **metal**. Molybdenum is found as an **ore**, combined with **sulfur**. It has a very high melting point, so it is used as a heat-resistant material.
Molybdenum is used in steel alloys.

monsoon   *noun*
A monsoon is a kind of **wind** that brings heavy rain. Monsoons occur in **tropical** regions and mark the change from the dry to the wet **season**.
The monsoon brought a very heavy rain that washed away the crops.

moonstone   *noun*
Moonstone is a kind of semiprecious stone. It has pale, shiny **crystals** and is often used in jewelry. Moonstone is a form of the mineral **feldspar**.
The moonstone shone in the candlelight.

94

moor *noun*

A moor is an area of high, open land where shrubs, such as heather, grow. Moors are found mainly in regions with a damp, temperate **climate**, such as northwest Europe. The soil contains much **peat**.
England is famous for its moors.

moraine *noun*

Moraine is a word that describes the **rocks** and **gravel** carried along by a **glacier**. When a glacier melts, the moraine is left behind as small mounds and hills. These are also called moraines.
The ground was very stony because the field was on a moraine.

mountain *noun*

A mountain is a piece of land that is much higher than the surrounding countryside. Mountains usually have steep sides and sharp or rounded **peaks**. Mountains are higher than **hills**. High mountains always have snow at the top.
We climbed up from the lowlands to the highest mountain in the chain.

mountain chain *noun*

A mountain chain is a series of mountains connected together. The Pyrenees form a mountain chain between France and Spain.
The peaks of the mountain chain rose up in the distance.

mountain range ► mountain chain

mouth *noun*

The mouth is the part of a river where the water flows out into the sea or a lake. The mouth of a cave is the entrance.
They played on the beach by the mouth of the river.

mud *noun*

Mud is a mixture of **clay**, **silt**, and water. Mud is found at the bottom of rivers, lakes, and **estuaries**. The **soil** of fields turns to mud after heavy rain. Many animals live in mud and some water plants are rooted in mud.
The mud on the road made driving difficult.

mud flat *noun*

A mud flat is a piece of land near the **seashore** that is covered by the sea at high **tide**. A mud flat is made up of **silt** or **clay**. It contains **channels** that are made by the sea when it runs back through the mud.
Many birds feed on the mud flat.

mudstone *noun*

Mudstone is a kind of **sedimentary** rock or **stone**. Mudstones are made of **clay** and **silt**.
Mudstones were found along the sides of the quarry.

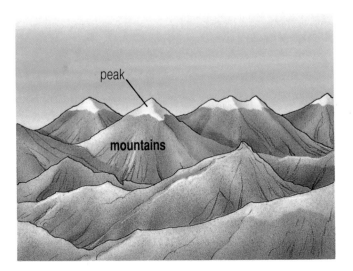

peak

mountains

95

natural *adjective*
Natural describes something that has not been made or altered by the activities of people. Natural vegetation describes plants that have not been disturbed by people or farm animals.
There was natural forest left in the valley.
nature *noun*

natural gas *noun*
Natural gas is a mixture of **gases**, mainly **methane** and small amounts of other **hydrocarbons**. Natural gas is very often found under the ground with deposits of **crude oil**. It is a **fossil fuel**.
Natural gas is used to heat homes.

natural resource *noun*
A natural resource is any useful substance found naturally. **Fossil fuels**, such as **coal**, **oil**, and **natural gas**, are examples of natural resources. **Forests** are a natural resource and are used as a source of timber. Many **nonrenewable** natural resources need to be managed carefully so that they are not used up.
The underground oil field was a valuable natural resource.

naturalist *noun*
A naturalist is someone who studies the wild plants and animals of a region.
Naturalists study the trees of the forest.

nautical *adjective*
Nautical describes anything having to do with ships, sailors, or **navigation**.
The ship was outfitted with the most modern nautical equipment.

navigation *noun*
Navigation is a word that describes how a ship or boat is guided across the sea, a plane through the skies, or a vehicle along roads.
Ships rely on accurate navigation.

neap tide *noun*
A neap tide is a **tide** with a small difference in water level between high tide and low tide. Neap tides occur when the **gravities** of the Sun and the Moon pull in different directions. Neap tides occur about every 14 days. The opposite of a neap tide is a **spring tide**.
Currents are weaker during neap tides.

neck ► plug

needle *noun*
A needle is a pointed piece of rock rising up from the sea. Needles are found close to sea **cliffs**, but separate from the cliffs. A needle is also the name for a mass of rock standing alone on a mountain.
Many sea birds nest on needles.

nekton *noun*
Nekton describes all those animals which can swim freely in the open sea. Animals of the nekton do not drift with the **tides** and **currents**, unlike the **plankton**, but can move in any direction. They range in size from a fraction of an inch long to many feet long. The nekton does not include the animals of the **benthos**, or sea floor.
Fish make up a large part of the nekton.

neon   *noun*
Neon is a colorless **gas** found in very small amounts in the **atmosphere**. It is an **inert** gas so it does not easily form **compounds** with other **chemicals**. Neon is used to fill some kinds of electric light bulbs.
The street was lit by neon lamps.

nephrite   *noun*
Nephrite is a **mineral** containing **silica**. It can be found in a variety of colors including black, white, yellow, and green. One form of **jade** comes from nephrite.
Nephrite is used in many types of jewelry.

neutral   *adjective*
Neutral describes a substance that is neither an **acid** nor an **alkali**. Pure water is neutral, and so is normal soil. Many plants will only grow well on neutral soil.
Lime can be added to acid soil to make it neutral.

névé   *noun*
Névé is recent **snow** that does not melt. The snow gradually turns to **ice** as it builds up on the ground. Névé is found high up on mountains, **glaciers**, or on snowfields in the **polar** regions.
The névé on the glacier turned slowly into ice.

nickel   *noun*
The **element** nickel is a **metal** that is found in many **ores** and is used to make many different **alloys**. The **core** of the Earth contains large amounts of nickel.
The alloy of nickel is harder than iron.

nimbostratus   *adjective*
Nimbostratus describes a kind of **cloud** that forms high up and looks like a dark gray sheet across the sky. Nimbostratus clouds cover the Sun and often produce continuous rain or snow. (See illustration page 30.)
The nimbostratus clouds hid the Sun.

nitrogen   *noun*
Nitrogen is the most common **gas** in the **atmosphere**. It makes up about 78 percent of the air. Nitrogen is necessary for the growth of animals and plants. **Compounds** of nitrogen are used as **fertilizers**.
Nitrogen was spread on the fields to make them fertile.

noble ► **inert**

nodule   *noun*
A nodule is a piece of hard **rock** that is found in softer, **sedimentary** rock. Nodules are also found on some parts of the seabed, and are rich in **iron** and **manganese** ores.
Many nodules have been found on the floor of the Pacific Ocean.

nodules

non-   *prefix*
Non- is a prefix that means not, changing the original word to the opposite meaning.
Carbon and oxygen are nonmetallic elements because they are not metals.

nonferrous   *adjective*
Nonferrous describes substances that do not contain **iron**. **Aluminum** is a nonferrous metal but steel is not.
The machine was made of nonferrous metal.

nonporous   *adjective*
Nonporous describes substances that do not let water through. Hard rocks that do not have cracks or gaps in them are nonporous. Solid **clay** is also nonporous. The opposite of nonporous is **porous**.
The nonporous rocks held water in a hollow.

nonrenewable   *adjective*
Nonrenewable describes **natural resources** that cannot be replaced once they have been used. **Oil** and **coal** are nonrenewable **fossil fuels**. **Wood** is renewable, if trees are planted to replace those that are cut down.
People are now learning to conserve the Earth's nonrenewable resources.

North Pole   *noun*
The North Pole is the most northern region on the **Earth**. There are two north poles: the geographical North Pole and the **magnetic pole**.
The North Pole is about 1,060 miles from the magnetic north pole.

northern hemisphere   *noun*
The northern hemisphere is the half of the **Earth** that lies to the north of the **Equator**. North America, Europe, and Asia lie in the northern hemisphere.
The plane from Australia crossed the Equator into the northern hemisphere on its flight path to North America.

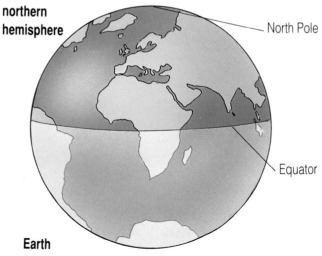

oasis   *noun*
An oasis is a fertile area with a good water supply in a **desert**. An oasis may be a very small area around a **spring**, or it may cover a whole valley floor. The water in an oasis allows trees and crops to grow.
The caravan crossed the desert and reached the oasis.

obsidian   *noun*
Obsidian is a kind of **igneous** rock with a dark colour and a **glass**-like texture.
The rocks near the volcano contained patches of glassy obsidian.

ocean   *noun*
An ocean is a very large **sea**. The five oceans on Earth are the Pacific, Atlantic, Indian, Arctic, and Southern oceans. Together, the oceans cover 71 percent of the Earth's surface.
The ship took many days to cross the ocean.

ocean basin   *noun*
The ocean basin is part of the **ocean floor** in areas where the **ocean** is more than 6,500 feet deep. It is the gently sloping or flat part of the floor between **oceanic ridges**.
The underwater mountain sloped down toward the ocean basin.

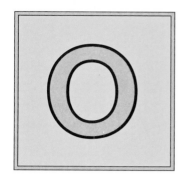

ocean current *noun*
An ocean current is a regular movement of **sea water** in the surface of the seas or **oceans**. Ocean currents follow particular routes. The Gulf Stream, which flows northward in the Atlantic Ocean, is an example of an ocean current.
The boats were helped on their way by the strong ocean current.

ocean floor ► page 100

oceanic climate ► **maritime**

oceanic crust *noun*
The oceanic crust is the inner and denser part of the Earth's **crust**. It lies beneath the **oceans**, but also partly continues beneath the **continents**. The oceanic crust is about 3 miles thick. It is made largely of **sima**.
The rocks below the oceans form part of the oceanic crust.

oceanic ridge *noun*
An oceanic ridge is an underwater **range** of **mountains**. The ridges wind their way around the **ocean floor** for many thousands of miles. Most mountains in the oceanic ridges stand about 5,000 feet above the ocean floor. The best known oceanic ridge is the Mid-Atlantic Ridge in the Atlantic Ocean. (See illustration page 100.)
The bed of the ocean rose up sharply toward the oceanic ridge.

oceanographer *noun*
An oceanographer studies the **oceans** of the world. Some oceanographers study the physical and **chemical** properties of the oceans, while others study its marine life.
Oceanographers explain how the ocean currents move chemicals around in the seas.

oceanography *noun*
Oceanography is the study of everything having to do with **oceans**.
Oceanography includes the study of marine life.

offshore *adjective*
Offshore describes something that moves away from the **seashore** or that is situated out to sea. An offshore **breeze** is a breeze blowing from the seashore away from the land and out to sea. The opposite of offshore is **onshore**.
The sailing boat picked up speed in the offshore wind.

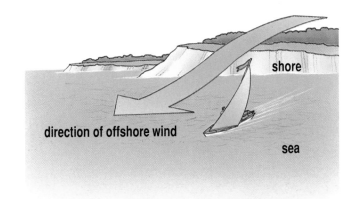

shore

direction of offshore wind

sea

oil *noun*
Oil is a thick, dark liquid that is made of **hydrocarbons**. Oil is a kind of **fossil fuel** formed over millions of years from the remains of plants. **Crude oil** is usually found underground with **natural gas** and solid hydrocarbons. Oil can also be extracted from some forms of shale and sand. An area containing reserves of oil is called an **oil field**. Oil and oil products are sometimes called petroleum.
The well pumped up the oil from deep underground to the surface.

oil field ► page 104

Oligocene *adjective*
Oligocene describes an **epoch** in **geological time**. It is one of the epochs of the **Tertiary** subera lasting from about 38 million years ago until about 24 and a half million years ago. (See chart page 64.)
Some scientists think that the first apes appeared on Earth during the Oligocene Epoch.

ocean floor *noun*

The ocean floor is the name given to the bottom of the **oceans**. The deepest part of the ocean floor is called the **abyssal plain**. From the abyssal plain, the ocean floor rises upward toward the **continents**. The ocean floor is made of rocks, covered by layers of mud.

The wrecked ship sank down through the water until it rested on the ocean floor.

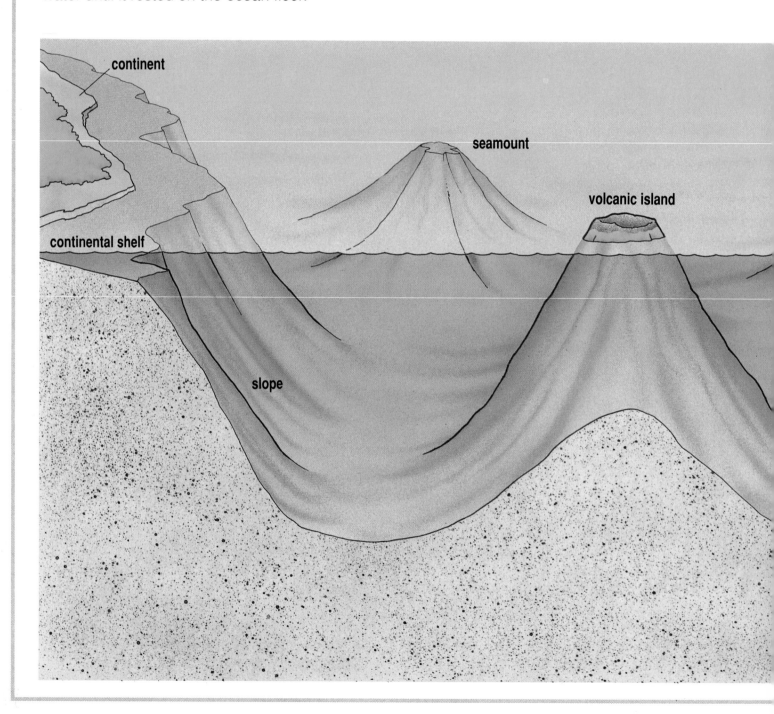

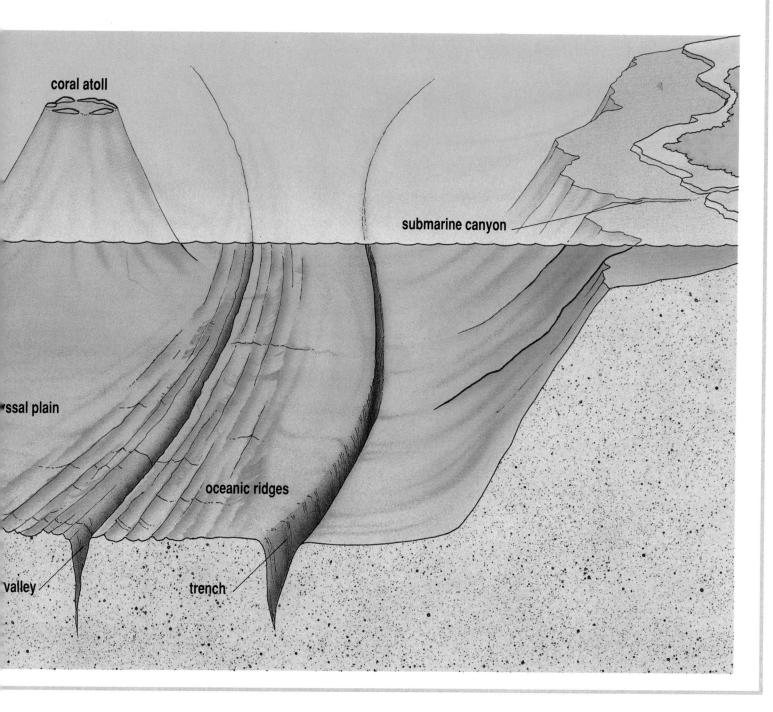

coral atoll

submarine canyon

ssal plain

oceanic ridges

valley

trench

onshore *adjective*
Onshore describes something that is at the **seashore** or that moves toward the seashore. An onshore **breeze** is a breeze blowing toward the seashore from the sea. The opposite of onshore is **offshore**.
The strong onshore wind quickly blew the boat into the port.

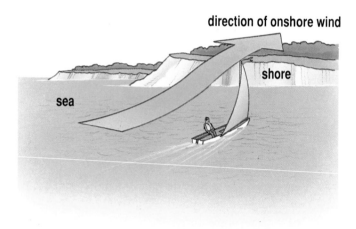

direction of onshore wind

shore

sea

onyx *noun*
Onyx is a **mineral**. It is a form of **chalcedony** that contains **opal**. Onyx is a semiprecious stone similar to **agate**.
His ring contained a brown-and-white onyx stone.

ooze *noun*
Ooze is a kind of slimy **sediment** found on the **ocean floor** made of the remains of **plankton**, animals, and plants mixed with **clay** and **silt**.
The submarine collected samples of the ooze at the bottom of the sea.

opal *noun*
Opal is a **mineral**, a form of **silica** and a semiprecious stone. Opals can be white or they may have **rainbow** colors.
Some of the finest opals come from Australia.

opisometer *noun*
An opisometer is an instrument for measuring distances on a **map**. A wheel traces a line on the map while a **scale** measures the distance that the wheel has traveled.
An opisometer can be used to measure how far one walks.

orbit *noun*
An orbit is the path followed by an object as it circles another object in space. The Earth follows an orbit around the Sun. Satellites and space stations circle the Earth in orbits.
The spaceship followed an orbit around the Earth.

Ordovician *adjective*
Ordovician describes a **period** in **geological time** from about 505 million years ago until about 438 million years ago. (See chart page 64.)
The geologist showed us a fossil coral from the Ordovician Period.

ore *noun*
An ore is a naturally occuring combination of **minerals**, especially useful **metals**, such as **gold**, **tin**, or **iron**. Pure metals can be **extracted** from large quantities of ore.
The train brought loads of iron ore to the foundry.

organic *adjective*
Organic describes a group of chemical **compounds**. Organic **chemicals** are those that contain atoms of **carbon**. Organic chemicals are often composed of carbon atoms joined together in chains or rings. All living things are made of organic chemicals. The opposite of organic is **inorganic**.
The biologist explained that animals and plants contain organic compounds.

osmium *noun*
Osmium is an **element**. It is a hard, brittle **metal** that has a bluish-white color. It is similar to **platinum** and is often found in the same ores as platinum.
They used osmium to make the hard tips of the pen points.

outcrop *noun*
An outcrop is an area of land where the **bedrock** comes to the surface. An outcrop may be of exposed rocks, or it may be covered with soil and plants.
We noticed different flowers growing on the limestone outcrop.

outer core *noun*
The outer core is part of the interior of the **Earth**. It lies inside the **mantle**, about 1,400 miles below the surface of the Earth. The outer core is very hot. It is thought to be made of **molten** rocks, with large amounts of **nickel** and **iron**. (See page 43.)
The outer core surrounds the Earth's magnetic inner core.

oxbow lake *noun*
An oxbow lake is a shallow **lake** found beside a **river**. Oxbow lakes are curved in shape. They form at a deep **meander** or bend in a river. When the river changes its course, the meander silts up and forms an oxbow lake. In North America, oxbow lakes are called bayous. (See illustration page 123.)
The oxbow lake was almost overgrown with water plants.

oxide *noun*
An oxide is a chemical **compound** that forms when an **element** reacts with **oxygen**. **Iron** reacts with oxygen in the air to make iron oxide, or rust.
The car's exhaust gave out poisonous oxides.

oxygen *noun*
The **element** oxygen is a common, colorless **gas**. One-fifth of the Earth's **atmosphere** is oxygen. Oxygen is the most common element in the Earth's **crust**. Nearly all living things need oxygen to survive.
The waterweed was covered with bubbles of oxygen.

ozone *noun*
Ozone is a type of **oxygen** and a colorless **gas**. It is formed when oxygen is exposed to **radiation**, especially in the upper **atmosphere**. Ozone is poisonous to breathe in large quantities.
Scientists monitor the ozone in the air.

ozone layer *noun*
The ozone layer is the name for part of the Earth's **atmosphere**. It is about 13 miles above the Earth's surface and is part of the **stratosphere**. The ozone layer protects the Earth from the harmful **radiation** of the Sun. Certain **gases** called chlorofluorocarbons, or CFCs, may damage the ozone layer.
The chemicals that collected in the air began to thin the ozone layer.

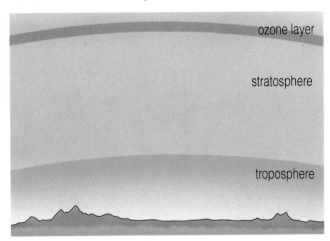
ozone layer
stratosphere
troposphere

oil field   *noun*

An oil field is a large underground **deposit** of **crude oil**. Oil fields are found in **sedimentary rocks**, often thousands of feet below the surface of the Earth. There are large oil fields in the Middle East and in the United States.

It was necessary to drill through layers of rocks to reach the oil in the oil field.

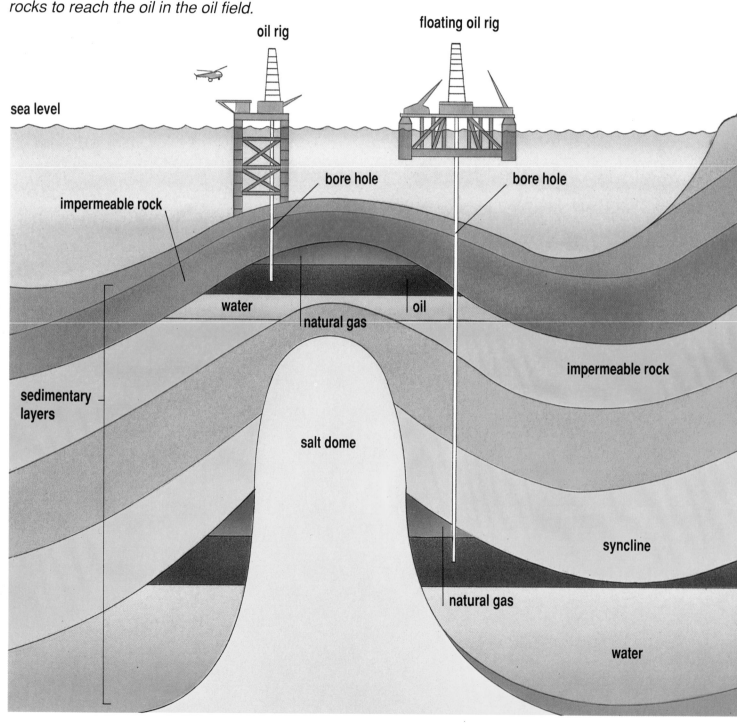

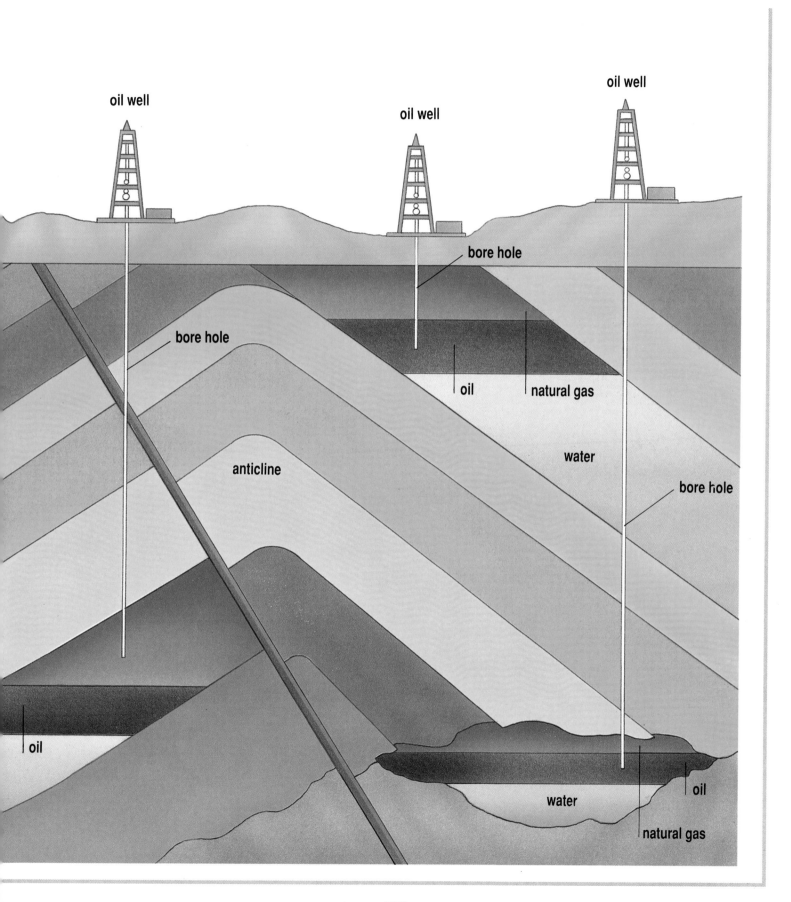

oil well

oil well

oil well

bore hole

bore hole

oil

natural gas

water

anticline

bore hole

oil

water

oil

natural gas

paleo- *prefix*

Paleo- is a prefix meaning old or ancient.
The science of paleontology studies life in the distant past.

Paleocene *adjective*

Paleocene describes one of the **epochs** of the **Tertiary** subera lasted from about 65 million years ago until about 55 million years ago. (See chart page 64.)
The Paleocene Epoch begins at the start of the Tertiary subera.

paleogeography *noun*

Paleogeography is the study of the **geography** of the Earth in earlier **geological time**. A student of paleogeography tries to determine what the Earth was like millions of years ago by studying **fossils** and **rocks**.
Paleogeography can provide important clues about the conditions for life in the past.

paleontologist *noun*

A paleontologist studies **fossils**. Some paleontologists collect and describe fossils. Others use the fossil traces left by extinct animals and plants to help them reconstruct the animal or plant.
Many paleontologists study fossils in a museum.

paleontology *noun*

Paleontology is the study of **fossils**. Paleontology can also be the study of the processes in **geology** that led to the formation of the fossils.
The study of dinosaurs is part of paleontology.

Paleozoic *adjective*

Paleozoic describes one of the **eras** in **geological time**. The Paleozoic Era lasted from about 590 million years ago until about 248 million years ago. (See chart page 64.)
In the middle of the Paleozoic Era, the first land plants appeared.

pampas *noun*

The pampas is a kind of **grassland** found in South America, mainly in Uruguay and Argentina. There are many tall grasses on the pampas and trees are scarce. The climate of the pampas is **temperate**.
Cattle range on the pampas.

Pangaea ► page 108

panning *noun*

Panning is a simple method used for separating precious **metals** from **gravel**. Panning is mostly used to search for **gold**. A person panning for gold sieves the gravel of a **stream** or **river** and then picks out any pieces of gold by hand.
Panning was a common method of retrieving gold during the California Gold Rush.

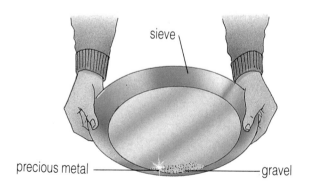

sieve

precious metal ———— gravel

Panthalassa   *noun*
Panthalassa is the name of the large **ocean** that some scientists believe surrounded the **supercontinent** of **Pangaea**. Panthalassa may have existed between about 250 million years ago and 215 million years ago. (See chart page 108.)
The map illustrated the position of the huge sea called Panthalassa.

parallel   *noun*
A parallel is another name for a line of **latitude**.
The ship sailed across several parallels as it traveled north.

pass   *noun*
A pass is a narrow path or channel, usually an area of lower ground through **hills** or **mountains**. A pass connects one **valley** with another valley.
The hikers climbed over the pass and then walked down into the valley beyond.

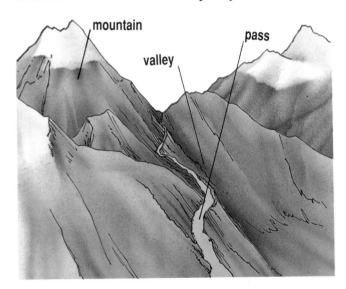

peak   *noun*
A peak is the highest point of a **mountain**. Some mountains have several peaks close together. Other mountains have a single peak. Mount Everest, in the Himalayas in Asia, rises to a peak at a height of 29,028 feet above **sea level**.
We could see the peak of the mountain rising above the clouds.

peat   *noun*
Peat is a kind of **soil**. It is produced under wet conditions in **bogs** from the decomposing remains of plants, mainly mosses, and has a dark brown color. Peat is a very good source of **humus** and can be dried and burned. It is an important source of fuel in some northern countries like Russia.
Sphagnum moss is one of the most important plants that form peat.

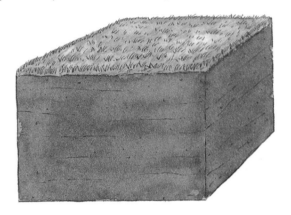

pebble   *noun*
A pebble is a small rounded piece of **rock** about a quarter of an inch across. They are often found on **beaches**.
We found it hard to walk across the stony pebbles.

pedology   *noun*
Pedology is the study of **soils**, including studying how different kinds of soil are made, and what the soils are made from. Pedology also involves making **maps** of different soils to show where they are found.
Pedology provides important information to those who work in agriculture.

pelagic   *adjective*
Pelagic describes substances or life forms found in the open water of the **sea** or in a large **lake**. Pelagic fish spend their lives swimming in the open sea or in the surface waters. Pelagic animals include the **nekton** and the **plankton**, but not the **benthos**.
A net can be used near the water's surface to catch pelagic fish.

Pangaea *noun*

Pangaea is the large land mass, or **supercontinent**, that some scientists think existed about 250 million years ago. According to the theory of **plate tectonics**, they believe that all the land in the world may have been joined together in the supercontinent of Pangaea, which broke up about 215 million years ago. The continents moved slowly apart, drifting to their current locations.

Triassic Period
Before 215 million years ago

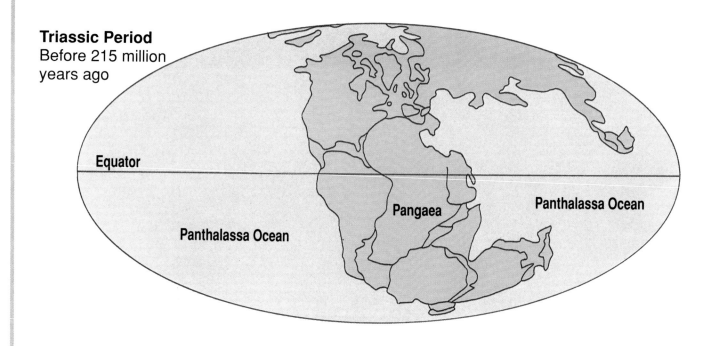

Jurassic Period
After 215 million years ago

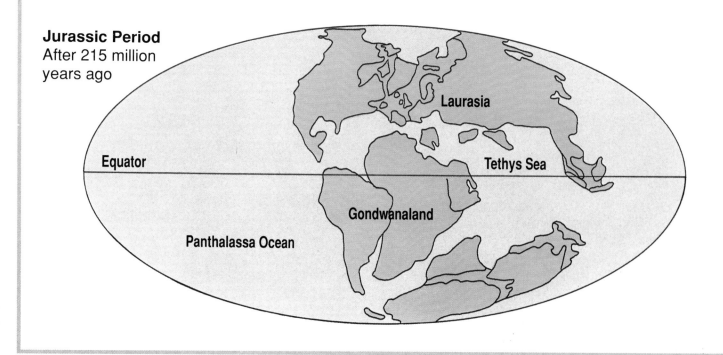

Cretaceous Period
Before 65 million
years ago

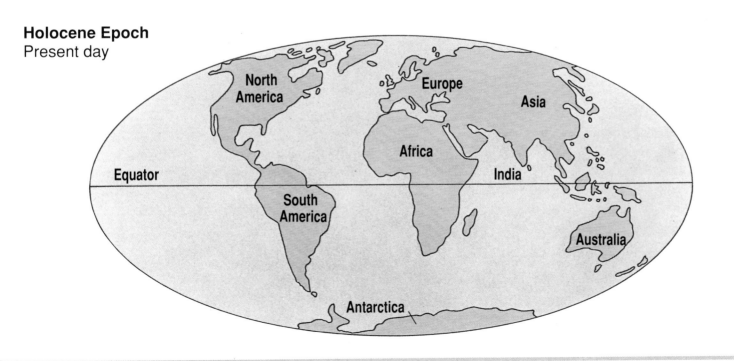

Tethys Sea

Equator

Holocene Epoch
Present day

North
America

Europe

Asia

Africa

India

Equator

South
America

Australia

Antarctica

peneplain *noun*
A peneplain is a kind of fairly flat **plain** of very old rocks which have been worn away by millions of years of **erosion**. Some of the best developed peneplains are found in southern Africa and in Brazil.
The old rocks formed part of an ancient peneplain.

peninsula *noun*
A peninsula is a narrow area of **land** that stretches out into the sea or a **lake**. A peninsula can be small, or very large like the Malay Peninsula in Southeast Asia.
Baja California forms a peninsula at the base of North America.

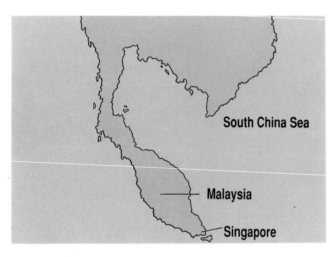

Pennsylvanian *adjective*
Pennsylvanian is used in North America to describe a subperiod in **geological time**. The Pennsylvanian includes the later part of the **Carboniferous** Period from 320 million years ago to about 286 million years ago. (See chart page 64.)
Coal began to form during the Pennsylvanian subperiod.

peridot *noun*
Peridot, or olivine, is a **mineral** made of **silica**, **iron**, and **magnesium**. Peridot is hard and glassy, with an olive-green color. Good **crystals** of peridot are used as **gems**.
The stones included some pale green crystals of peridot.

peridotite *noun*
Peridotite is an **igneous** rock with a very coarse grain. Peridotite is common in the Earth's **mantle** and often contains the mineral **peridot**.
The rock in the area contained evidence of peridotite.

period *noun*
A period is one of the main divisions of **geological time** beginning 590 million years ago. Each **era** is divided into several periods. Each period is divided into **epochs**. (See chart page 64.)
Layers of coal formed in the Carboniferous Period.

periodic table *noun*
The periodic table is a list of all the **elements** in order, from the lightest to the heaviest atomic weights.
Hydrogen is the element with the lowest atomic weight in the periodic table.

permafrost *noun*
Permafrost describes **ground** that is always frozen in regions which are very cold, such as the **Arctic**. In the Arctic **summer**, the **ice** on the surface of the ground melts while the ground below is still frozen. The soil gets very wet because permafrost below stops the water from draining away.
We could not dig through the permafrost.

permeable *adjective*
Permeable describes something through which **water** can pass. A permeable **soil** is a soil that allows free **drainage** of water. The opposite of permeable is **impermeable**.
Limestone rock is very permeable.

Permian *adjective*
Permian describes a **period** in **geological time** from about 286 million years ago to about 248 million years ago. The Permian Period is the first period of the **Paleozoic** Era. (See chart page 64.)
Ammonites lived during the Permian Period.

pervious   *adjective*
Pervious describes **rocks** through which water slowly passes. Water passes through a pervious rock by seeping along cracks and joints. Some limestone and some igneous rocks are pervious. The opposite of pervious is **impervious**.
The water dripped into the cave through the pervious rocks above.

petrified forest   *noun*
A petrified forest is a **forest** that has been turned into **fossils**. The wood in the trees is gradually replaced by **silica** from water that is rich in mineral **salts**. The most famous example is in the Petrified Forest National Park in the United States.
Stone-like fossil trees are preserved in the petrified forest.

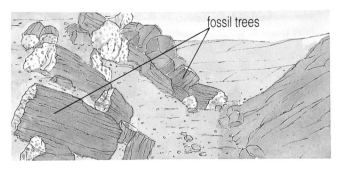
fossil trees

petroleum ► **oil**

petrologist   *noun*
A petrologist is a scientist who studies **rocks**. Petrologists identify different rocks from their structure and from the **chemicals** of which they are made. They also study the geological processes that make different types of rock.
Petrologists can detect minerals in rock.
petrology   *noun*

Phanerozoic   *adjective*
Phanerozoic describes the most recent **eon** in **geological time**. It began about 590 million years ago and continues today. (See chart page 64.)
All the geological periods have occurred during the Phanerozoic Eon.

phosphorus   *noun*
Phosphorus is an **element** found in many different types of **rock** and **mineral**, mainly as a **compound** with **calcium**. Phosphorus is used to make matches and **fertilizers**. All living things need phosphorus.
Crops can not grow unless there is enough phosphorus in the soil.

physical geography   *noun*
Physical geography is the study of the surface of **continents** and of **landscapes**. It includes looking at the way the landscape is formed by **erosion**, the flow of rivers, or **glaciation**.
The physical geography of the valley showed that it had once been filled with thick ice.

physical map   *noun*
A physical map is a **map** that shows details of the physical **features** of the **landscape**. A physical map can show any low and high ground, **rivers**, **lakes**, and **marshes**.
The mountains were indicated on the physical map.

piedmont   *noun*
A piedmont is a gentle **slope** found at the foot of a **mountain**, running down from the mountain to a **plain**.
They came down from the foothills onto a broad piedmont.

piedmont

pipe   *noun*
A pipe is a tube-shaped opening in a solid substance, such as the **vent** through which **lava** rises into the **crater** of a **volcano**. It can also describe a hole in rock that is filled with a different rock or **mineral**.
The geologist found diamonds in a pipe.

pitchblende *noun*
Pitchblende is an **ore** of **uranium**. It is very **radioactive** and has a black color. Uranium and **radium** are obtained from pitchblende.
Radium was first extracted from pitchblende.

plain *noun*
A plain is a flat area of **lowlands**. The plains of East Africa are covered with trees and **grasslands**. The Great Plains of North America are used for growing grain crops. Many plains stretch for hundreds of miles.
The grassland stretched away across the open plain.

planet *noun*
A planet is a large mass that travels around the **Sun**. There are nine planets in our **solar** system. The **Earth** is the third closest planet to the Sun and takes one year to travel around it. Planets can be made of **rocks** or **gases**. The Earth is made of rocks and is surrounded by an **atmosphere**.
The Earth is the only planet known to support living things.

plankton *noun*
Plankton is the name for the tiny animals and plants that float in the **water** or in the **air**. They cannot control their movements, but drift along on **currents**. Marine plankton are found in the upper layers of the sea. Aerial plankton include tiny insects and spiders which get swept up in air currents. Many plankton can only be seen with a microscope. Creatures that can swim freely are called **nekton**.
The fish fed on the plankton in the sea.

marine plankton

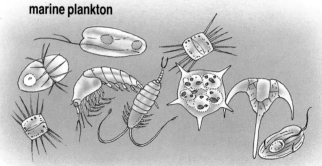

plate ► **tectonic plate**

plate tectonics *noun*
Plate tectonics is the study of movements in the Earth's **crust**. The crust is thought to be divided into a number of **tectonic plates** that move and push against each other. There are seven large plates and twelve smaller ones. One plate can move under another in a **subduction zone**. When plates move apart, **sea-floor spreading** will occur. The plates can also slide past each other without any change to their size. (See illustrations page 34 and 142.)
The study of plate tectonics shows that the continents are slowly moving.

plateau (plural **plateaux**) *noun*
A plateau is a raised area of flat ground surrounded by steep **slopes** or **escarpments**. Most plateaux lie above 2,000 feet. The Tibetan plateau lies at a height of about 13,000 feet.
The village was built overlooking the edge of a high plateau.

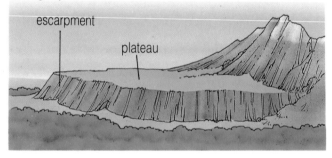

platinum *noun*
The **element** platinum is a silvery **metal**. Platinum is normally found combined with **sulfur**. It is rare and valuable, and used to make jewelry.
Some rings are made of platinum bands.

Pleistocene *adjective*
Pleistocene describes an **epoch** in **geological time**. It occurred in the **Quaternary** subera and lasted from about 2 million years ago to about 10,000 years ago. (See chart page 64.)
Many glaciations took place during the Pleistocene Epoch.

Pliocene *adjective*
Pliocene describes an **epoch** in **geological time**. It is the last epoch in the **Tertiary** subera and lasted from about 5 million years ago to about 2 million years ago. (See chart page 64.)
Icecaps developed during the Pliocene Epoch.

plug *noun*
A plug is a mass of solid **lava** in the **vent** of a **volcano** that is **dormant** or **extinct**.
Sometimes, a plug is left exposed when the softer rock surrounding it erodes away.
The castle was built high up on an old plug.

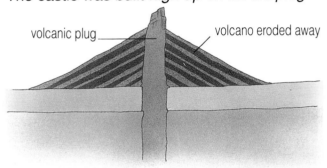

volcanic plug   volcano eroded away

plutonium *noun*
Plutonium is a **radioactive element**. It is not found naturally as an **ore** but is made in nuclear reactors from **uranium**. Plutonium is mainly used as a nuclear **fuel**.
The waste from the nuclear reactor contained high levels of plutonium.

polar *adjective*
Polar describes something that comes from or that is found close to the **North Pole** or **South Pole**. Polar air is cold air moving from the polar regions.
The explorers set out to cross the polar ice.

pole *noun*
The poles of the Earth are the points at its extreme north and south. The **North Pole** and the **South Pole** are directly opposite each other. They are known as the geographical poles. The North Pole is over the frozen **Arctic** Ocean. The South Pole is over the ice-covered **continent** of **Antarctica**.
Many expeditions were lost trying to reach the Earth's poles.

pollute *verb*
Pollute means to add **impurities** or unwanted substances, especially to the **environment**. Untreated sewage can pollute **rivers**. Factories may pollute the **atmosphere** with smoke and the water with waste **chemicals**. **Acid rain** pollutes land and water.
The oil spill polluted the sea over a wide area.
pollution *noun*

polonium *noun*
The **element** polonium is a **radioactive metal**. Polonium is found naturally with **uranium** in **pitchblende**.
The scientists measured the radioactivity of the polonium carefully.

porcelain *noun*
Porcelain is a hard, white substance used to make objects such as cups and saucers. It is made from kaolin, **feldspar**, and **quartz**, which are heated together at a high **temperature**.
He carefully washed the valuable porcelain.

porous *adjective*
Porous describes something through which water is able to pass. **Gravel** is very porous, as are **soils** that contain a lot of **sand** or **organic** matter.
The porous soil dried out quickly after the heavy rain.

porphyry *noun*
Porphyry is any **igneous** rock that has large **crystals**.
The sculpture was chiseled out of porphyry.

projection *noun*

Projection is a process used in **map**-making. Since it is very difficult to draw a flat map of a round world, only one part of the map will be drawn to a correct **scale**. Other areas of the map will be stretched or reduced in size to fit. The different ways of altering the shapes to fit the flat map are called projections.

The projection used in the map made Greenland seem as large as South America.

cylindrical projection

Cylindrical projection fits a map onto a cylinder shape. The scale of the map is correct along the Equator, but gets more and more stretched as it approaches the poles. Cylindrical projection is most often used for maps of areas on either side of the Equator.

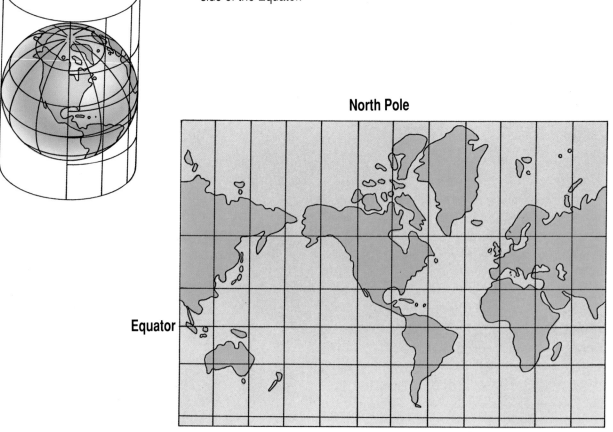

North Pole

Equator

conical projection

Conical projection fits a map onto a cone shape. The scale of the map is correct along the **meridians**, but only correct along one or two chosen lines of **latitude**. Conical projection is good for making maps of countries with large areas of land running east and west.

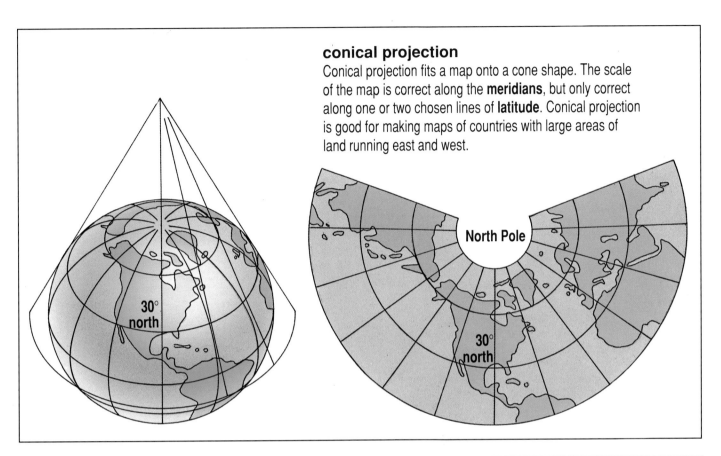

azimuthal projection

Azimuthal projection fits a map onto a flat shape. The scale of the map is correct where the flat shape and the curve of the Earth melt. Azimuthal projection can be used for mapping areas such as the poles.

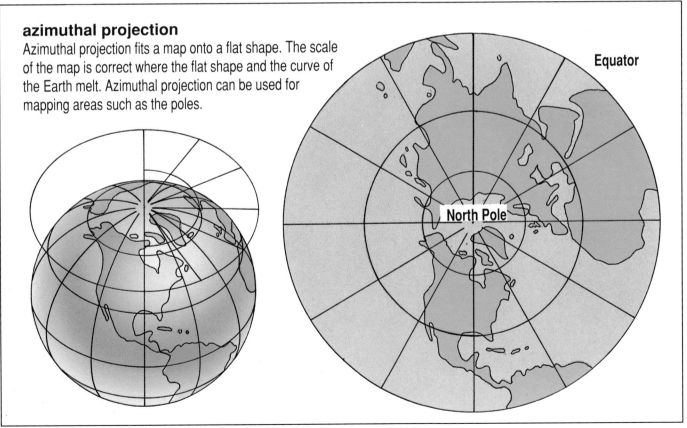

potash *noun*
Potash is a **compound** of **potassium** made of potassium carbonate and other potassium **salts**. Potash is found with other salts, such as common salt, in **salt lakes**. It is also found in ash. Potash is used as a **fertilizer** for plants.
Potash can be added to garden soil to help plants grow.

potassium *noun*
Potassium is an **element**. It is a **metal** that is found in many **minerals**, and also in sea water. All living things need some potassium to grow.
Cooking salt contains potassium.

pothole *noun*
A pothole is a smooth-sided, round hole in the rocky bed of a **stream**. A pothole forms when the water swirls **pebbles** around in a shallow dip, gradually eroding the dip until it becomes a pothole. A pothole is also the shaft where a stream runs into an underground limestone **cave**.
The stream flowed into a large pothole.

prairie *noun*
The prairie is the treeless, grassy **plain** in the center of the North American **continent**. On the prairie, the rain falls mostly in the **summer**, when it is also hot. In the **winter**, it is dry and cold.
We rode on horseback over the open prairie.

Precambrian *adjective*
Precambrian is a name sometimes used for the earliest part of **geological time**. It includes the **Priscoan**, **Archean**, and **Proterozoic** eons. It lasted from about 4,600 million years ago until about 590 million years ago. Many ancient rocks date from Precambrian times. (See chart page 64.)
The center of the continent was made of Precambrian rocks.

precipitation *noun*
Precipitation is the **water** that falls from the **atmosphere** onto the Earth's surface. It includes **snow**, **sleet**, **hail**, and **dew** as well as **rain**.
The ground was wet from the precipitation.

pressure *noun*
Pressure is the force of the **atmosphere** or **water** on the Earth. **Atmospheric pressure** is lower at the top of a mountain than at **sea level**. Water pressure increases at lower and lower depths in the sea.
A sudden change in atmospheric pressure may mean a change in the weather.

pressure gradient *noun*
A pressure gradient is the difference in **pressure** between two points. There is a steep pressure gradient between an area of **high pressure** and one of **low pressure**. A steep pressure gradient, with strong winds, is marked on a weather chart by **isobars** placed close together. Widely-spaced isobars show a weak gradient and light winds.
The wind reached gale force as the pressure gradient rose.

prevailing wind *noun*
The prevailing wind in an area is the **wind** that blows there most often. At different seasons of the year, the direction of the prevailing wind may change.
The prevailing wind blew from the west coast of the continent.

prime meridian ► **Greenwich meridian**

Priscoan *adjective*
Priscoan is the earliest **eon** of **geological time**. Some scientists think that it dated from 4,600 million years ago to 4,000 million years ago. The Priscoan Eon is the earliest part of **Precambrian**. (See chart page 64.)
Some scientists think that the Earth was formed during the Priscoan Eon.

projection ► page 114

promontory ► **headland**

Proterozoic *adjective*
Proterozoic describes the **eon** in **geological time** from about 2,500 million years ago to about 590 million years ago. The Proterozoic Eon is the later part of **Precambrian** time. (See chart page 64.)
Life first appeared in the sea during the Proterozoic Eon.

pumice *noun*
Pumice is a kind of **igneous** rock and a kind of **lava**. It is formed from frothy, **molten** rock that cooled down so quickly it did not form crystals. It is very light because it has a sponge-like structure and is full of holes. Pumice is used as an **abrasive**. Some pumice even floats on water.
We found pieces of pumice near the volcano.

pyrite *noun*
Pyrite is a **mineral** made of **iron** and **sulfur**. Crystals of pyrite are very shiny and have a gold color and are sometimes called fool's gold. It is found in **sedimentary** and **igneous** rocks.
Pyrite is mined as a source of sulfur.

quagmire *noun*
A quagmire is an area of very soft, wet **ground**. It is difficult to walk on a quagmire because of the danger of sinking.
We had to take a different route to avoid the quagmire.

quarry *noun*
A quarry is an open pit made by digging for rocks or **minerals**. The surface soil is removed to reach the rocks or minerals below. Stone for building and **slate**, **sand**, and **gravel** are dug from quarries.
The slates for the new roof came from the local quarry.

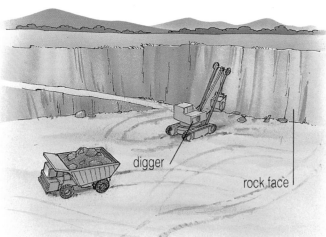

digger

rock face

quartz *noun*
Quartz is a **mineral**. When it is pure, quartz is transparent and colorless. Quartz is made of **crystals** of **silica** and is hard enough to scratch glass. There are many different types of quartz, and it is the most common mineral in the rocks of the Earth.
The pale quartz showed up clearly among the darker rocks.

Quaternary   *adjective*
The Quaternary subera is the most recent of all **geological time**, and includes the **Pleistocene** and **Holocene** epochs. It began about 2 million years ago and continues to the present day. (See chart page 64.)
We are still living in the Quaternary subera.

quicksand   *noun*
Quicksand is very wet **sand** found in some **estuaries**. Quicksand becomes more liquid when it is pressed so it is dangerous to walk over.
The farmer had to pull the cow out of the quicksand with a rope.

radiation   *noun*
Radiation is a kind of **energy**. It includes the particles given off by **elements** that are **radioactive**. Some radiation is harmful if it is accidentally absorbed in large doses and can destroy living cells.
The nuclear power station had very thick walls to contain the radiation.

radioactive   *adjective*
Radioactive describes **elements** that give off **radiation**. Some elements, such as **uranium** and **radium**, are naturally radioactive.
Scientists can calculate the age of radioactive rocks.
radioactivity   *noun*

radium   *noun*
Radium is an **element**. It is a **radioactive metal** found in ores such as **pitchblende**. Radium decays to form the gas **radon**.
The scientist used radium as a source of radiation.

radon   *noun*
Radon is an **inert** gas found in small quantities in the **atmosphere**. Radon is given off when the metal **radium decays**.
Radon trapped in the air in a home can be dangerous.

rain   *noun*
Rain is **water** that falls in drops from the **clouds**. The biggest raindrops fall as **thunderstorms** or heavy showers. The smallest drops are drizzle.
The travelers were soon soaked by the heavy rain.

rain forest   *noun*
A rain forest is a special kind of **forest** with tall trees and many climbing plants. Rain forests are found in **tropical** regions where the climate is always warm and there is a high **rainfall**. Central America, South America, Africa, and Southeast Asia have many rain forests. The largest is the Amazon rain forest in South America.
Many animals, such as monkeys, snakes and parrots, live in the rain forest.

rainbow   *noun*
A rainbow is an arch of colors seen in the sky. The six main colors in a rainbow are red, orange, yellow, green, blue, and violet. When **sunlight** shines through **rain**, the raindrops split up the sunlight into these colors.
The rainbow appeared in the sky over the fields.

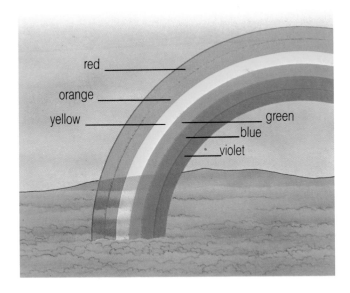

rainfall   *noun*
Rainfall is the amount of **rain** that falls, usually measured in inches per year. Some parts of the world have a very high rainfall, which causes **floods**. In places where there is not enough rainfall, there may be a **drought**.
The heavy rainfall brought enormous floods, which caused widespread damage.

range   *noun*
A range is a series of objects in a line, such as **mountains** or **hills**. Range is also used to describe open, rolling country, such as the **prairie** in North America.
The mountain range was covered in snow.

rapids   *noun*
Rapids are very fast-flowing parts of a **river**. In the rapids, the **water** rushes quickly over a series of **waterfalls**.
The rapids made the river very dangerous.

rare earth   *noun*
A rare earth is a kind of **element**. Rare earth elements are found in small quantities in **minerals**. Although they are called rare earths, some of these substances can be found quite easily.
The rock from the moors contained rare earths.

ravine   *noun*
A ravine is a deep, narrow river **valley** that is formed when rivers rush over rocks and wear away a **channel**. A ravine is similar to a **gorge**, but the sides are less steep.
The hikers climbed carefully along the ravine.

reef *noun*

A reef is a line of hard **rocks** or **coral** at or near the surface of the sea. **Coral reefs** form in warm water around volcanic **islands**. In time, the volcano may disappear beneath the water, and the reef can become an **atoll** with a **lagoon** in the center.

Reefs can be very dangerous obstacles for boats and ships.

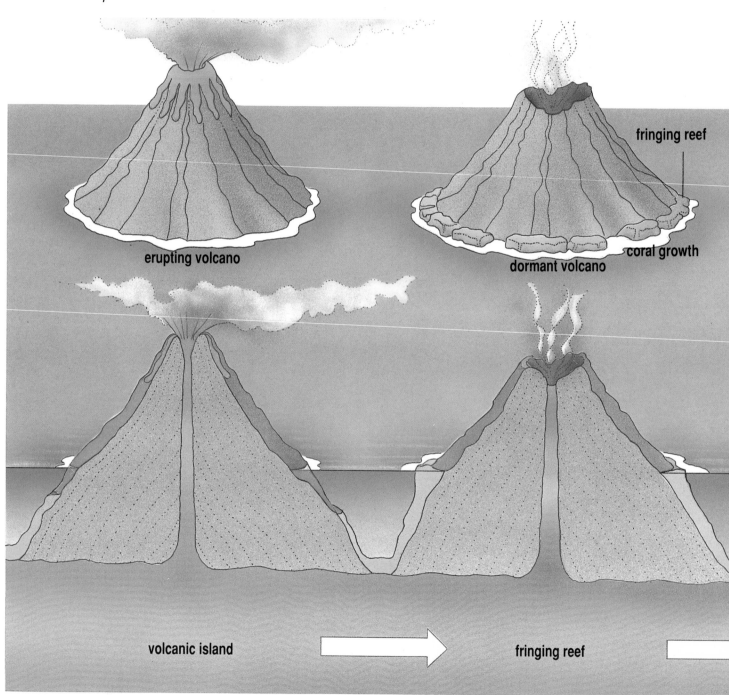

erupting volcano

fringing reef

dormant volcano

coral growth

volcanic island

fringing reef

The four stages of reef development are illustrated below. The top pictures show what the reefs look like above the water. The bottom pictures are a cross-section of the reefs displaying what is happening under the water and inside the volcano or reef.

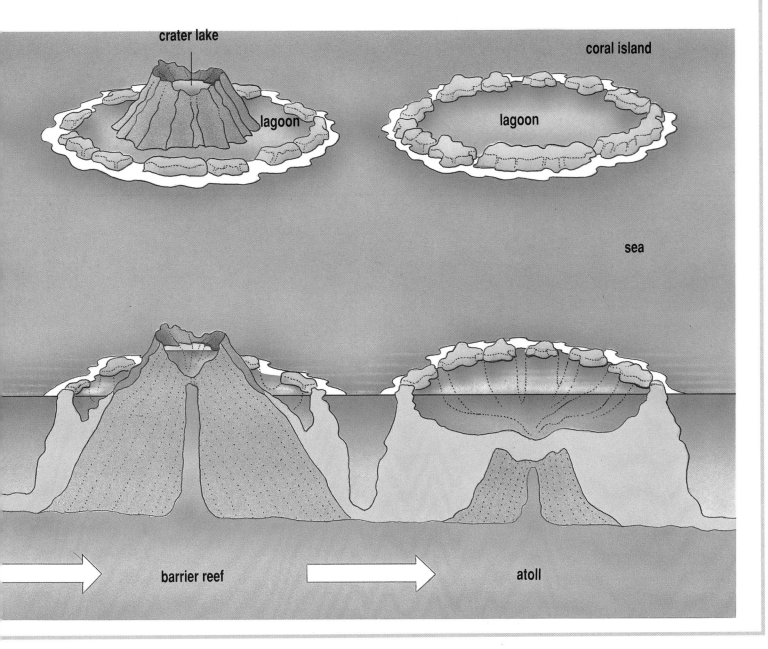

river *noun*

A river is a large stream of **water** that flows along a **channel** called a **river bed**. The **source** of a river is high in hills and mountains, usually at a spring or a lake. Rivers flow down toward the sea, collecting more water and growing gradually wider and slower.

The longest rivers flow for thousands of miles.

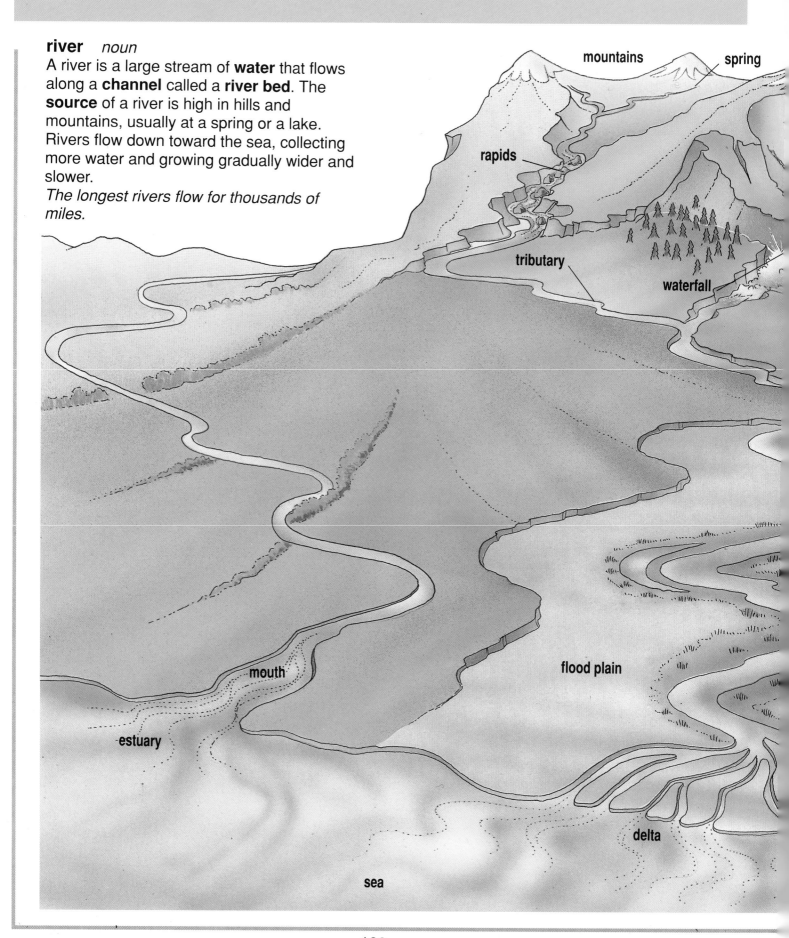

mountains

spring

rapids

tributary

waterfall

mouth

flood plain

estuary

delta

sea

glacier

snow

source

alluvial fan

meander

oxbow lake

red clay *noun*
Red clay is a kind of **clay** formed deep in the **oceans**. It is made up of fine particles that are carried by **ocean currents** to the deepest parts of the sea.
Red clay covers the deepest ocean floors.

reef ► page 120

reg *noun*
A reg is a kind of **desert** with a flat surface covered in **gravel**. Wind has swept away any small particles of loose **sand**.
There are many large areas of reg in the Sahara in North Africa.

region *noun*
A region is an area of **land**. Some regions are flat, while others are hilly. Each region has certain **features** that distinguish it.
There were many lakes in the region.

relative humidity *noun*
Relative humidity is a measure of **moisture** actually in the **atmosphere** compared to how much moisture air at that temperature can hold before **precipitation** occurs. If the relative humidity is very high, **mist**, **fog**, or **rain** can occur. The relative humidity is usually lower during the day than during the night. It is measured with a **hygrometer**.
The fog was caused by the relative humidity.

relief map *noun*
A relief map is a **map** that shows the **features** of the **landscape**. The areas of high and low ground can be shown by **contours**, different colors or shading.
The relief map showed a range of hills.

reservoir *noun*
A reservoir is an artificial **lake** that stores water that is used for drinking or for **irrigation**. Most reservoirs are made by stopping river water behind a **dam**. A deposit of **crude oil** can also be called a reservoir.
Our drinking water came from a reservoir nearby.

resource ► **natural resource**

Richter Scale *noun*
The Richter Scale measures the strength of **earthquakes** and earth **tremors**. The Richter Scale goes from 0 to 9. Strong earthquakes measure over 7 on this scale.
The earthquake measured more than 6 points on the Richter Scale.

ridge *noun*
A ridge is a narrow, raised stretch of **land**. **Hills** and **mountains** that are close to each other are often joined together by a ridge.
There was a valley on each side of the ridge.

rift valley *noun*
A rift valley is a long, deep **valley** formed when part of the Earth's **crust** collapses along a **fault** line. The African Rift Valley is the largest known, stretching northward from the Zambezi River in Africa to the Middle East.
There was a long line of lakes at the bottom of the rift valley.

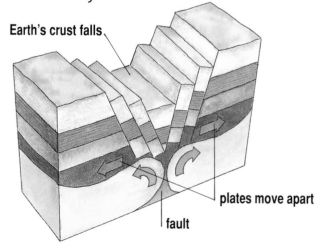

Earth's crust falls

plates move apart

fault

rime ► **hoarfrost**

river ► page 122

river bed   *noun*
A river bed is the base of the **channel** in which a **river** flows. It is made of rocks and mud and it may contain many kinds of water plants and animals.
The level of water was so low that we could walk along the river bed.

rock   *noun*
Rock is the term used for hard **mineral** deposits. The Earth's **crust** is made of solid rocks about 40 miles deep. Rocks are named according to the way they were formed. The main types of rock are **igneous**, **metamorphic**, and **sedimentary**. Small, individual rocks are called **stones**. (See illustration page 136.)
The well was drilled through solid rock.

rock formation   *noun*
A rock formation is the shape given to **rocks** by **wind**, **water**, and heat. All over the world, wind and water have **eroded** rocks into unusual shapes, while cooling **igneous** rock produces quite different rock formations. Rock formations can be a major **feature** of the landscape.
There can be many different types of rock formations in a single landscape.

ruby   *noun*
A ruby is a precious stone that can be used as a **gem**. Rubies are a form of the mineral **corundum**. A ruby is red because it contains very small amounts of **chromium**. Many rubies come from mines in Burma.
Rubies are valuable gemstones.

runoff   *noun*
Runoff is that part of the **rainfall** that reaches the **streams** and **rivers**. The rest either **evaporates** back into the **air** or seeps into **rocks** under the ground.
There is more runoff after a heavy rain.

saline   *adjective*
Saline describes a liquid that contains **salt**. **Sea water** is a liquid that is saline, because it contains common salt.
A saline solution can be used as a disinfectant.

salinity   *noun*
Salinity is a measure of the amount of any **salt** that is dissolved in water. All water, even fresh water, contains some salt. **Sea water** has a high salinity because it contains a large amount of salt. Some **lakes** have even higher levels of salinity than sea water.
A high salinity gives water a very strong salty taste.

salinization   *noun*
Salinization is the process by which a **soil** absorbs more and more **salt**. **Evaporation** removes the water from the soil, leaving the salts behind. If there is too much salt in the soil, it becomes **infertile**, and crops will not grow. Salinization is common in the soil near the **coast** in warm regions and in the soil in dry regions.
The crops failed to grow in the soil because it had been affected by salinization.

salt   *noun*
A salt is a kind of chemical **compound** formed when an **acid** and a base react together. There are many different salts. Common salt, or sodium chloride, is the most widely known. It is found in sea water and can also be found underground as rock salt.
Salt may be added to food to bring out the flavor.

salt lake   *noun*
A salt lake is a **lake** with a high **salinity**. Salt lakes form in hot, dry regions when water **evaporates** from the lake, leaving the salts behind. The Dead Sea, in Israel, is a famous salt lake.
The water in the salt lake is so salty that people can float easily.

salt marsh   *noun*
A salt marsh is an area of wet **ground** near the **coast** that is sometimes flooded by the sea. When the sea floods the ground, the water becomes salty.
The salt marsh attracted many wild birds.

salt pan   *noun*
A salt pan is a small **salt lake**. Common salt can be collected from salt pans. The water in a salt pan **evaporates** in the sun and wind, and the salt is left behind as **crystals**.
Large quantities of salt were obtained from the salt pans on the coast.

salt water   *noun*
Salt water is **water** that contains a high level of dissolved **salts**. The **oceans** and seas and some inland **lakes** contain salt water.
They knew they were near the sea because the river contained salt water.

sand   *noun*
Sand is a kind of **detritus** made up of tiny grains of **minerals**, such as **quartz**. Sand is often found at the **coast**. Over many hundreds of years, the **waves** of the sea grind down the rocks into sand. Sand particles are smaller than a twelfth of an inch across.
Children use damp sand to make castles.

volcanic sand

quartz sand

sand from red sandstone

sand dune ► dune

sandbank   *noun*
A sandbank is a mound of **sand** that is found in the **sea**, an **estuary**, or a **river**. When a water **current** that is carrying sand slows down, the sand falls through the water and is deposited as a mound. Sandbanks can be a danger to boats as they can usually be seen only at low **tide**.
The ship ran aground on the sandbank that was hidden below the water.

sandbank

sea

sandbar   *noun*
A sandbar is a narrow **sandbank** at the mouth of a river or **estuary**.
Several seals were basking in the sun on the sandbar.

sandstone   *noun*
Sandstone is a kind of **sedimentary** rock or **stone** made of sand grains held tightly together by **mud**. Sandstone is easy to cut and shape, and is often used for building. Sandstone is often a red color.
The island was ringed by sandstone cliffs.

sandstorm   *noun*
A sandstorm is a strong **wind** that carries grains of **sand**. In a sandstorm, sand and **dust** may be lifted to a great height and carried many miles. Sandstorms are common in sandy **deserts**.
The expedition found travel difficult in the fierce sandstorm.

sapphire *noun*
A sapphire is a precious stone with a bright blue color. A form of **corundum**, sapphire is almost as hard as **diamond**.
A huge sapphire sparkled at the center of the woman's necklace.

savanna *noun*
Savanna is a kind of dry, lowland **plain** found in the **tropics**. In a savanna, there are patches of **grassland** with scattered bushes and trees.
The lions moved across the open savanna in search of antelopes.

scale *noun*
Scale is a measure used to show the size of features shown on a **map**. The scale of a map compares the size of the details shown on the map with the actual size of the features. A scale is also a set of regularly spaced marks, used for measuring. A thermometer has a scale marked in **degrees**, for measuring temperature. The **Beaufort Scale** measures the force of the wind.
We could see many details on the map because it was drawn on a large scale.

scarp ► **escarpment**

schist *noun*
Schist is a kind of **metamorphic** rock. In schist, the surface of the rock is very flaky and shiny. The mineral **mica** is a common type of schist.
Shiny bands of schist were visible in the rock face.

scree *noun*
Scree is a collection of loose **rocks** and **stones** on the side of a **mountain**. It is formed by the **weathering** of a rock face. Usually, the larger pieces of rock are at the base of the pile, with smaller stones higher up. Heaps of scree can often be seen at the foot of **cliffs** and steep **slopes** in mountainous country.
He walked very carefully over the scree to avoid losing his footing on the loose rocks.

scrub *noun*
Scrub is the name for a dry habitat with many small bushes. Sometimes, scrub grows up after a **forest** has been cut down. Other types of scrub are found where there is not enough **rainfall** to allow trees to grow.
They traveled a long way through the scrub to reach the river.

sea *noun*
The sea is the great mass of **salt water** that covers more than three-quarters of the **Earth's** surface. Enormous areas of the sea are known as **oceans**.
The huge waves of the sea crashed against the rocks at the coast.

sea level *noun*
Sea level is the average height of the surface of the **sea**. The height of land is measured from sealevel.
The floods spread quickly because the land was below sea level.

sea stack ► **needle**

sea water *noun*
Sea water is the water in the **sea**. Most sea water is very salty because that it contains **salts** of **sodium**, **calcium**, and **magnesium**.
At the mouth of the river, the fresh water mixed with sea water.

seabed *noun*
The seabed is the bottom of the **sea**. Like dry land, the seabed can be flat or can have huge **mountain** ranges and deep **valleys**.
The divers explored the seabed.

sea-floor spreading *noun*
Sea-floor spreading describes the movement of the Earth's **crust** at the **seabed**. Molten rock, or **lava**, comes to the surface at the **mid-oceanic ridges**. The rock is then pushed out sideways, making the sea-bed wider. The study of sea-floor spreading is part of **plate tectonics**.
The scientists measured the amount of sea-floor spreading on the sea-bed.

seam *noun*
A seam is a band of a **mineral** trapped between two layers of **rock**. **Coal** is often found in long seams.
The miners removed the coal by working straight along the seam.

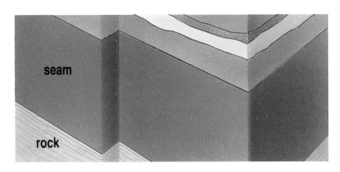

seamount *noun*
A seamount is a single volcanic **mountain** rising up from the **seabed**. Although they are far below **sea level**, seamounts can be over 11,500 feet high. Seamounts do not appear above the surface of the water.
The seamount rose up steeply from the flat ocean floor.

seashore *noun*
The seashore is the land immediately next to the **sea**. Many seashores are covered with **sand**, but they may also be rocky or covered with **shingle**.
We searched the seashore for different kinds of rock.

season *noun*
A season is a part of the year that has a particular **climate**. In **temperate** regions, the four seasons are **spring**, **summer**, **autumn**, and **winter**. These vary in both **temperature** and **rainfall**. In the **tropics**, there are usually two seasons. These are the hot, dry season and the hot, rainy season.
It can rain almost constantly during the rainy season.

seaway *noun*
A seaway is a safe way over the ocean that has been drawn on a **chart** for ships to follow. It is also a very wide, deep canal.
The seaway took the ship safely past the islands.

sediment *noun*
Sediment is the solid that settles at the bottom of a liquid. **Stones** and **mud** gather as sediment at the bottom of **rivers**, **streams**, and on the **seabed**.
The bed of the lake was covered in sediment.

sedimentary *adjective*
Sedimentary describes a type of **rock** or **stone** that is formed from **sediments**. Some such as **breccia**, are formed from small pieces of other types of rock. Others such as **chalk**, are made up of the **shells** of tiny animals.
The quarry contained sedimentary rock.

sedimentology *noun*
Sedimentology is the study of **sedimentary** rocks. Sedimentology helps in the exploration for **oil**, **natural gas**, and **coal**.
Sedimentology is important in the mining industry.

seismic wave   *noun*

A seismic wave is a wave of **energy** that travels through the **Earth** from an **earthquake**. Seismic waves spread out from the **focus** of an earthquake and can cause much damage. They are felt as **foreshocks**, **aftershocks**, or **tremors** on the land. At sea, a seismic wave may produce a huge tidal wave called a **tsunami**.
Scientists use precise instruments to record the strength of seismic waves.

seismograph   *noun*

A seismograph is an instrument that measures how much the **ground** shakes or vibrates. A pen records **seismic waves** on paper fixed to a moving drum. It can also record movements caused by explosions.
The geologist recorded the distant earthquake on a seismograph.

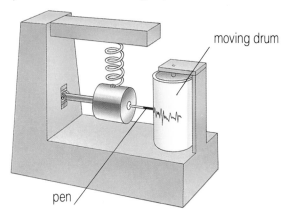

moving drum

pen

seismology   *noun*

Seismology is the study of **seismic waves**. It gives us information about **earthquakes**, the structure of the **Earth**, and activity in the Earth's core.
Seismology can be used to predict earthquakes.

serpentine   *noun*

Serpentine is a **mineral** found in **igneous** rocks. Serpentine is normally dark green, but it can also be brown, yellow, or white. Serpentine can be carved and polished to make ornaments.
On the desk, there was a dark, shiny paperweight made of serpentine.

settlement   *noun*

A settlement is formed when a group of people set up, or establish, a new village or town. A settlement is also any collection of dwellings. Some settlements are as large as a city. Other settlements are as small as a few huts in the brush.
The fishermen built a settlement by the sea.

sextant   *noun*

A sextant is an instrument used to measure the angle of the Sun, the Moon, or the stars from the horizon. Sailors at sea can work out their **latitude** with a sextant.
The sextant helped the ship's captain calculate the position of the nearest island.

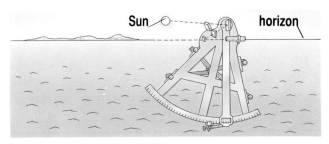

Sun   horizon

shaft   *noun*

A shaft is a straight tunnel going into the ground. Many **mines** are made by digging shafts.
The miners had to travel down the shaft to reach the ore.

shale   *noun*

Shale is a kind of **sedimentary** rock formed when **clay** and **silt** deposits turn to rock. It is brittle and breaks easily.
The cliffs were too dangerous to climb because they were formed from shale.

shell *noun*
A shell is the hard, outer covering of some animals. Shells are made mostly of **calcium**. Some kinds of **limestone**, such as **chalk**, are made of tiny shells that have been crushed and packed tightly together.
He found many cowrie shells on the beach.

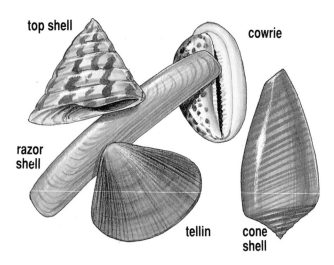

top shell
cowrie
razor shell
tellin
cone shell

shield *noun*
A shield is part of the Earth's **crust**. It is a large area of old **metamorphic** and **igneous** rocks of **Precambrian** age. These rocks are flat because they have not been folded or buckled into **mountains**.
The rocks of the Canadian shield are some of the oldest rocks in the world.

shingle *noun*
Shingle is **pebbles** or coarse **gravel** found on **beaches**. The stones in shingle are between about a half inch and three inches across. They are smooth because they have been **eroded** by the **waves**.
Over millions of years, the action of the waves will turn the shingle into sand.

shoal *noun*
A shoal is a bank of **sand** or **mud** in a **river** or in the sea. Shoals form when slow-flowing river water deposits its **sediment** along its path.
The digging machines removed the shoals from along the river channel to allow the water to flow.

shock wave *noun*
A shock wave is a sudden **wave** of enormous pressure. Like sound waves, shock waves can travel through air, water, or the ground. Most shock waves are caused by **earthquakes**. Explosions and **thunder** can also cause shock waves.
The distant explosion caused a shock wave.

sial *noun*
Sial is the material that forms the **continental crust** underneath the continents. It is made mainly of **granite** and contains **silica** and **aluminum**.
The rocks of the continental crust are largely made up of sial.

sierra *noun*
A sierra is a **mountain chain** containing a number of **peaks**, such as the Sierra Nevada in Spain.
The mules carried the luggage slowly along the path that led over the sierra.

silica *noun*
Silica is the main **chemical** in the Earth's **crust**. It is made of **silicon** and **oxygen**. **Quartz**, **flint**, **opal**, and **sinter** are all forms of silica. Silica is used in making glass and cement.
The silica used in the glass factory was ground to a fine powder.

silicates *noun*
Silicates are the most common **minerals**. Silicates are compounds containing **silicon** and **oxygen**, with one or more extra **elements**.
Many of the Earth's rocks and minerals are silicates.

silicon *noun*
Silicon is a common **element** found in the Earth's **crust**. Most silicon is combined with **oxygen**, as **silica**. Brick, **cement**, and glass all contain silicon. Pure silicon is used in computers and other electrical devices.
Silicon is the second most common element after oxygen.

sill *noun*
A sill is a layer of **igneous** rock trapped inside another type of rock, such as **metamorphic** rock. A sill forms when **magma** flows inside the metamorphic rock and then becomes solid. A sill is often harder than the rock around it.
The sill of hard rock jutted out from the side of the cliff.

silt *noun*
Silt is a dust-like substance made up of tiny particles of **rock**. **Rivers** and **streams** carry silt, which settles on the river bed as **sediment**. Silt can build up in **reservoirs**.
The sunken boat was partly covered in silt.

Silurian *adjective*
Silurian describes the **period** in **geological time** from about 438 million years ago to about 408 million years ago. (See chart page 64.)
The first land plants appeared during the Silurian Period.

silver *noun*
Silver is an **element**. It is a white, shiny **metal**. Silver is commonly found as an ore together with **lead**, **zinc**, or **copper**. Silver is sometimes found in its pure form. It is used to make ornaments and to conduct electricity. Silver **compounds** are used to make film.
The photographic film in a camera contains silver.

sima *noun*
Sima is the material that forms the **oceanic crust** underneath the oceans. The sima layer also lies under the **sial** of the **continental crust**. It is made mainly of **basalt** and contains **silica** and **magnesium**.
The rocks of the sea-bed are made of sima.

sinkhole *noun*
A sinkhole is a steep-sided hole in the surface of the ground. Sinkholes are common in **limestone** areas, such as in **karst** landscapes. Water from streams and rivers may fall through sinkholes into a **cave** below.
The sinkhole led to a series of deep caves.

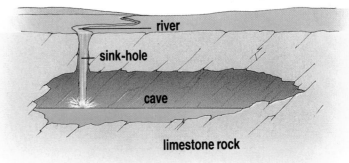

river
sink-hole
cave
limestone rock

sinter *noun*
Sinter is a **deposit** that is made of **silicates**. It is found around the edges of hot **springs** or **geysers**.
The sinter formed hard banks and ledges around the mouth of the geyser.

sirocco *noun*
The sirocco is a kind of warm, dry **wind** that blows northward from the Sahara toward the Mediterranean region.
We arrived in Italy as the sirocco began to blow.

slate *noun*
Slate is a kind of **metamorphic** rock or **stone** formed from **shale** or **mudstone**. Slate has a smooth surface and it splits easily in flat slabs. Slate is used for building and in roofing tiles.
When the gale blew, several pieces of slate fell from the roof.

sleet *noun*
Sleet is a mixture of **rain** and **snow**. Sleet can also be snow or **hail** that has partially melted and then falls from the sky.
Freezing sleet made traveling difficult.

slope *noun*
A slope is a piece of ground that rises or falls. On a **hill** or **mountain**, the slope is usually steepest near the top and becomes more gentle toward the bottom.
The walker looked for the path up the slope of the hill.

small-scale *adjective*
Small-scale is a term that describes a kind of **map**. A small-scale map covers a large area, but does not show much detail.
The small-scale map showed the mountain peaks but not the roads.

smog *noun*
Smog is a mixture of **fog** and smoke and other forms of pollution. Smog occurs in cities where fog is common and where there is much smoke in the air.
The thick smog settled over the city like a huge blanket.

snow *noun*
Snow is water that falls from **clouds** as **crystals** of **ice**. Snow forms when water **vapor** in the clouds turns directly into ice, without first becoming liquid.
The snow fell thickly and lay on the cold ground for weeks.

snowflakes

snow line *noun*
The snow line is the level on a **hill** or **mountain** above which the **snow** never melts. The height of the snow line varies with **latitude** and climate. It also depends upon the direction of the **wind** and the steepness of the slope.
The wolves came down below the snow line to hunt for food.

snowfield *noun*
A snowfield is a wide expanse of permanent **snow**. Snowfields are found in high mountains and around the **North Pole** and **South Pole**. Some snowfields may turn to ice and form **glaciers**.
The snowfield formed in a hollow in the rocks.

soapstone *noun*
Soapstone is a **mineral**. It is a smooth stone that feels soapy. Soapstone is a gray-green or brown form of **talc**. It can be carved easily and is used to make ornaments.
The tiny figure was carved from soapstone.

sodium *noun*
Sodium is an **element**. It is a **metal** that forms many important **compounds**, including common **salt** and bicarbonate of soda. Many **minerals** contain sodium.
Pure sodium makes water fizzy.

soft water *noun*
Soft water is **water** that does not contain **magnesium** or **calcium** salts. Soap in soft water lathers quickly and forms no scum. The opposite of soft water is **hard water**.
Only a small amount of soap powder is needed to wash clothes in the soft water.

soil *noun*
Soil is the layers of **earth** that lie on top of solid **rock**. Soil is a mixture of small pieces of rock, **minerals**, and **humus**. Most plants need soil in order to grow.
Farmers planted their crops in the best soil.

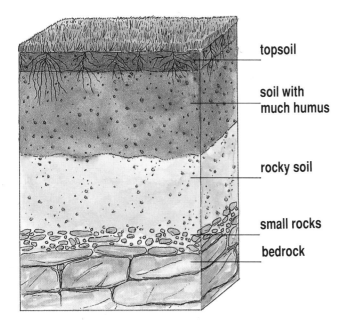

topsoil

soil with much humus

rocky soil

small rocks

bedrock

soil erosion *noun*
Soil erosion is the loss of **soil** from the surface of the ground. When the **wind** blows, dry soil may be blown away. Water can also cause soil erosion when heavy **rainfall** washes the soil away.
The farmers could no longer plant their crops because of the soil erosion.

solar *adjective*
Solar describes anything having to do with the **Sun**. Solar heat is heat that comes from the Sun.
The solar wind travels from the Sun at a speed of about nine hundred thousand miles an hour.

solar energy *noun*
Solar energy is energy that comes directly from the **Sun**. Solar energy can be used to make electricity and to heat water.
The house was heated using solar energy.

solstice *noun*
The solstice is the day in the year when the Sun reaches a position farthest north or south of the **Equator**. The Sun reaches its farthest north over the **Tropic of Cancer** on June 21st. It reaches its farthest south over the **Tropic of Capricorn** on December 21st. The position of the Sun seems to move from one side of the Equator to the other because of the rotation of the Earth on its **axis**.
The two solstices are called winter and summer solstices, depending on whether the days are getting shorter or longer.

sonar *noun*
Sonar is a system that uses sound waves to measure the depth of water. An instrument sends out pulses of sound, which bounce back off the **sea-bed**. The depth of water is measured on a depth scale. Shoals of fish can also be detected using sonar. Some forms of sonar are called **echo sounders**.
The scientists measured the depth of water in the channel using sonar.

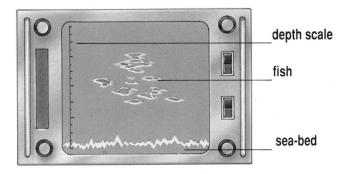

depth scale

fish

sea-bed

sound *noun*
A sound is a narrow **channel** of the **sea**. A sound usually runs between the mainland and an **offshore** island.
They watched the ships racing each other up the sound.

source *noun*
A source is the place where a **river** or **stream** begins to flow. A river runs from its source, which is often a **spring**, down to its **mouth** at an **estuary** or a **delta**.
The hikers followed the river to its source high up in the mountains.

South Pole *noun*
The South Pole is the area farthest south on the **Earth**. It lies close to the centre of the **continent** of **Antarctica**. There are two south poles. These are the geographical South Pole and the **magnetic pole**.
The Norwegian explorer Roald Amundsen reached the South Pole first, in 1911.

southern hemisphere *noun*
The southern hemisphere is the part of the **Earth** that lies south of the **Equator**. The **continents** of Australia and most of South America lie in the southern hemisphere.
The ship crossed over the Equator and sailed into the waters of the southern hemisphere.

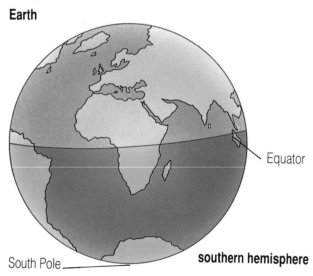

Earth

Equator

South Pole

southern hemisphere

speleology *noun*
Speleology is the study and exploration of **caves**. It includes the **geology** of caves, and the study of the animals and plants that live in caves.
Speleology may explain why bats make their homes in caves.

spit *noun*
A spit is a long, narrow stretch of **sand** or **gravel** running out into the **sea**. Spits form when water **currents** running along the seashore deposit sand and gravel. A spit often encloses an **estuary** or a **bay**.
The spit separated the sea from the river.

spring *noun*
A spring is the place where a **stream** or **river** rises out of the **ground**. Springs form above **impermeable** rock that lies at the surface of sloping ground.
The spring was the source of a large river.

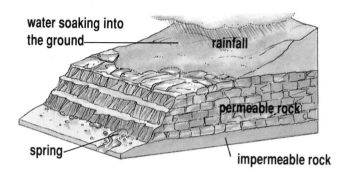

water soaking into the ground

rainfall

permeable rock

spring

impermeable rock

spring tide *noun*
A spring tide is a **tide** with a large difference in water level between high tide and low tide. Spring tides occur when the **gravities** of the Sun and the Moon pull in the same direction twice every month. The opposite of a spring tide is a **neap tide**.
The spring tide flooded the road.

squall *noun*
A squall is sudden, short, and rather violent **wind**. Squalls are common during **storms**.
They ran for shelter to avoid the strong squall.

St. Elmo's fire *noun*
St. Elmo's fire is a kind of **lightning**. It is a blue-green glow seen in the air during **storms**. It can sometimes be seen on the masts of ships at sea.
The sailors saw the St. Elmo's fire lighting up the clouds nearby.

stalactite *noun*
A stalactite is a pointed piece of **limestone** hanging down from the roof of a **cave** like an **icicle**. Stalactites are made of calcium carbonate. **Hard water** drips down and **evaporates**, leaving the calcium carbonate behind to form a stalactite. The opposite of a stalactite is a **stalagmite**.
Stalactites covered the roof of the cave.

134

stalagmite   *noun*
A stalagmite is a mound or spike of **limestone** rising up from the floor of a **cave**. **Hard water** falls onto the spike and **evaporates**, leaving calcium carbonate. The opposite of a stalagmite is a **stalactite**.
The stalagmite looked like a giant candle.

steppe   *noun*
A steppe is a dry, grassy **plain** without trees that is found in central Europe and Siberia. Steppes are found in **climates** that are too dry for trees to grow. Steppe **soils** are deep and fertile. In North America, these grassy plains are called **prairies**.
The farmers grew wheat on the fertile steppe.

stone ► page 136

storm   *noun*
A storm is a strong **wind** measuring force 10 or 11 on the **Beaufort Scale**. Some storms bring heavy **rain** and **thunder**.
The storm caused flooding, and damage.

strait   *noun*
A strait is a narrow strip of water connecting two **seas** or **oceans**. The Strait of Gibraltar connects the Atlantic Ocean with the Mediterranean Sea.
The boats followed each other in a line through the strait.

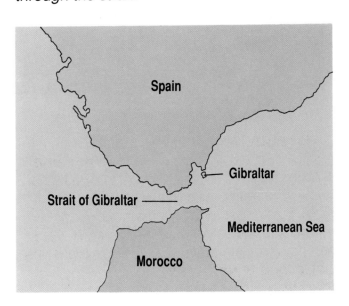

stratigraphy   *noun*
Stratigraphy is the study of the different **layers**, or **strata**, of **rocks**. In stratigraphy, a **geologist** can study the different rocks or **fossils** to determine when the rocks and fossils were formed.
The geologist used stratigraphy to calculate the age of the rocks.

stratocumulus   *adjective*
Stratocumulus describes a kind of gray and white **cloud**. These clouds form at a low level in the sky as a **warm front** passes. Stratocumulus clouds are rounded in shape. They often produce tiny drops of rain that fall as drizzle. (See illustration page 30.)
We expected rain when we saw the stratocumulus clouds approaching.

stratopause   *noun*
The stratopause is part of the Earth's **atmosphere**. It is the upper edge of the **stratosphere**, and lies at a height of about 30 miles above the surface of the Earth. (See illustration page 10.)
The temperature of the stratopause is about 0 degrees Celsius.

stratosphere   *noun*
The stratosphere is part of the Earth's **atmosphere**. It lies above the **tropopause**, and it is about 25 miles thick. This layer contains most of the **ozone** found in the atmosphere, and forms a protective shield preventing harmful **radiation** reaching the Earth from the Sun. There are very few **clouds** in the stratosphere. (See illustration page 10.)
The rocket passed through the stratosphere.

stratum (plural **strata**)   *noun*
A stratum is a **layer** in **sedimentary** rock. Strata vary in thickness from less than a half inch to many feet. They are normally horizontal. The word stratum is also used to describe any layer of the Earth's **atmosphere**.
We could see the bands of different strata on the cliff face.

stone *noun*

A stone is a hard, **mineral** deposit, a small piece of **rock**. Stones are formed from the three main types of rock: **igneous**, **metamorphic**, and **sedimentary** rock. *The three major ways in which stones can be made are shown below.*

stones made of metamorphic rock

stones made of sedimentary rock

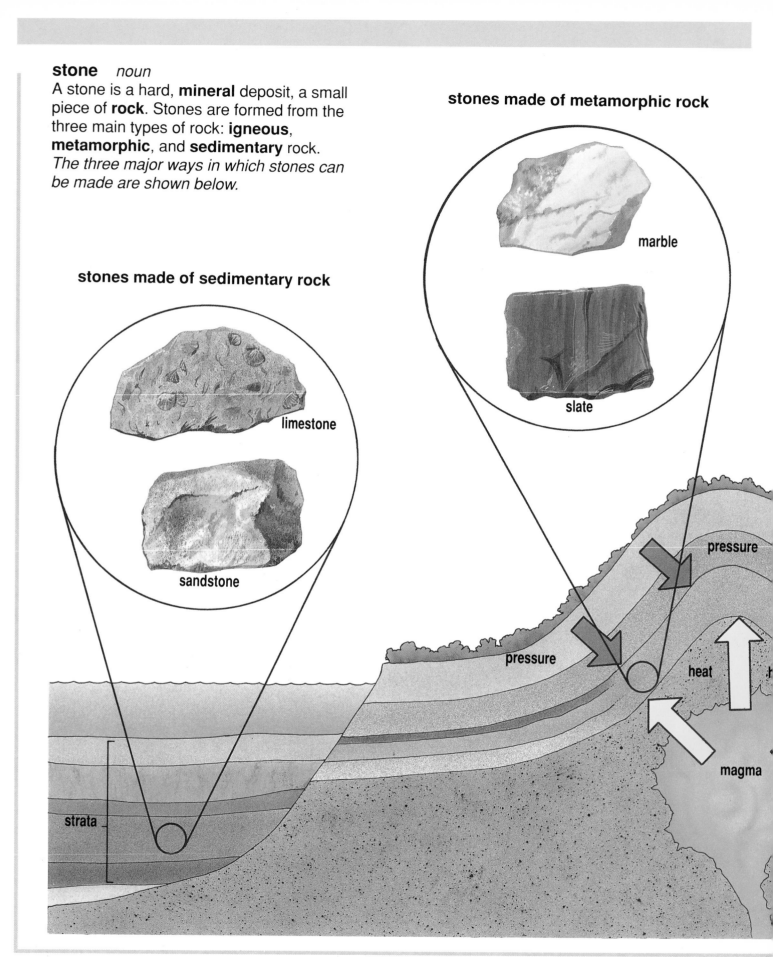

marble

slate

limestone

sandstone

pressure

pressure

heat

magma

strata

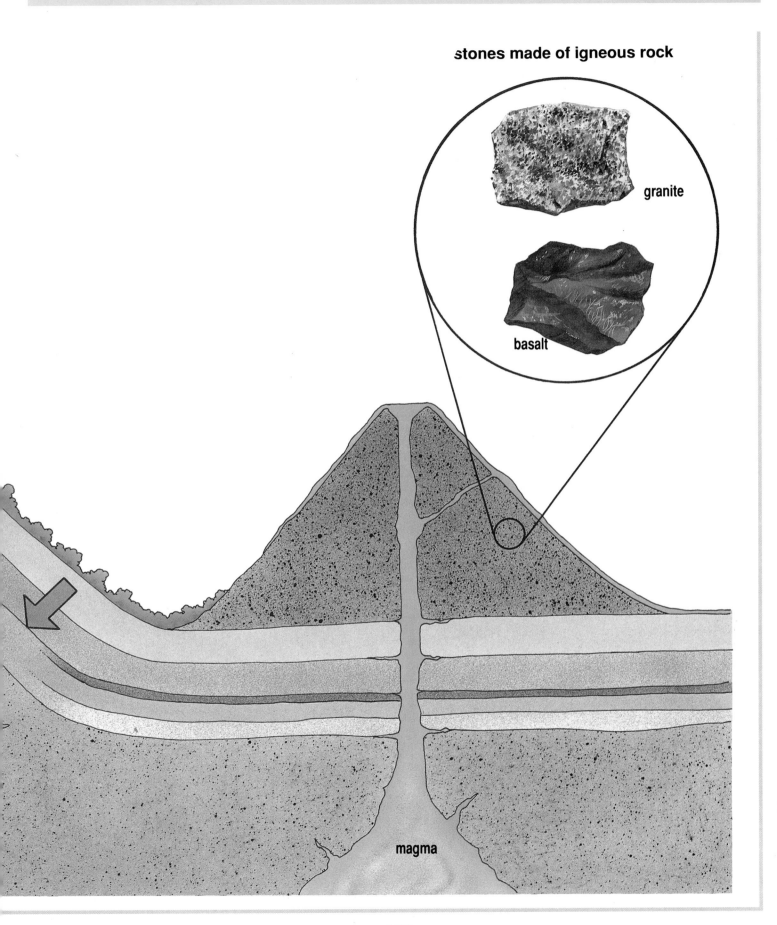

stones made of igneous rock

granite

basalt

magma

stratus *adjective*
Stratus describes a kind of **cloud** that forms when warm and cold air mix together. Stratus clouds form low in the sky. They are light gray with flat bases. Stratus clouds usually bring a fine, long-lasting rain. (See illustration page 30.)
It started to rain when the stratus clouds covered the whole sky.

streak color *noun*
The streak color is a feature of **minerals**. If a piece of a mineral is rubbed on a rough white surface, it will leave a colored mark, which may not be the same color as the mineral. Each mineral has its own streak color. **Geologists** use these streak colors to help them identify minerals.
We saw the mineral's characteristic streak color on the broken surface of the rock.

streak color

hematite

stream *noun*
A stream is a small **channel** of **water** that flows continually. Streams start at a **spring** or **lake** and join together to form **rivers**. Stream can also be used to describe a current or a continuous flow of a liquid or a gas, such as molten rock or air.
The stream flowed swiftly through the fields.

stress *noun*
Stress is strong pressure in the **rocks** or **soil** of the **Earth**. Stress is caused by movements in the Earth's **crust** that push rocks against each other. Stress causes rocks to bend and creates **faults** and **folds**. High levels of stress can also cause **earthquakes**.
The layers of rock had been bent by the stress in the ground below.

stria (plural **striae**) *noun*
A stria is a tiny groove or scratch on the surface of a **rock**. A stria is caused by the movement of ice, often during a **glaciation**. **Stones** and rocks in the ice at the bottom of a **glacier** scratch the rock below, leaving striae on the rock surface.
The geologist could tell which way the ice had moved by looking at each stria on the rocks.

sub- *prefix*
Sub- is a prefix that describes something under, below, or less.
The subsoil was dry and infertile.

subduction zone *noun*
A subduction zone is an area on the Earth's **crust** where a **tectonic plate** goes down into the **mantle**. Subduction zones lie below oceanic **trenches**. (See illustration page 34.)
The Earth's crust gradually disappeared along the subduction zone.

submarine *adjective*
Submarine describes an object or habitat that is found below the surface of the **sea**.
The aquarium contained a selection of submarine life.

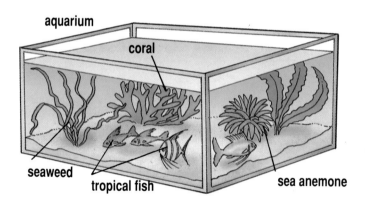
aquarium
coral
seaweed
tropical fish
sea anemone

submarine plain ▶ **abyssal plain**

submersible vehicle *noun*
A submersible vehicle is one that can move about under water. A **bathyscaphe** is one kind of submersible vehicle.
A submersible vehicle provides access to the seabed.

subsidence *noun*
Subsidence is a sinking of **earth** or **soil**. It can be caused by **rocks** and soils collapsing into a space below the ground, or caves and mines can collapse and cause subsidence.
The house could not be built over the old mine because the builders feared subsidence.

subsoil *noun*
Subsoil is the **soil** below the surface soil, or **topsoil**. The subsoil is less often disturbed than the topsoil and contains less **organic** material. The subsoil also has more **clay** and **minerals** than the topsoil. The subsoil lies above the **bedrock**.
The deep plow made a furrow right down to the subsoil.

subterranean *adjective*
Subterranean describes something that is below the **ground**. A subterranean **river** is a river that flows under the ground.
The path led down into a series of subterranean caves.

subtropical *adjective*
Subtropical describes two regions that lie near the **tropics**. One subtropical region reaches north from the **Tropic of Cancer** to **latitude** 40 degrees north, and the other subtropical region reaches south from the **Tropic of Capricorn** to latitude 40 degrees south.
Crops grew well in the subtropical climate.

sulfur *noun*
Sulfur is a greenish-yellow **element** in its pure form, and it is often found as **compounds**. With **oxygen**, it forms the poisonous **gas** called **sulfur dioxide**. Sulfur is used to make many things, including matches and medicines.
The volcano smelled strongly of sulfur long after it had erupted.

sulfur dioxide *noun*
Sulfur dioxide is a poisonous **gas** made when **chemicals** containing **sulfur** are burned. Smoke from chimneys often contains sulfur dioxide. It is one of the causes of **acid rain**.
We could smell the sulfur dioxide in the smoke from the factory.

summer *noun*
Summer is the name for the warmest **season** of the year in **temperate** climates. In the summer, the Sun is at its highest point in the sky and the days are longest. In the **northern hemisphere**, summer lasts from June to August. In the **southern hemisphere**, summer lasts from December to February.
By the time it was summer, the snow on the mountains had melted.

summit *noun*
Summit is the highest point of a **hill** or **mountain**. The summit of Mount Everest, the **Earth's** highest mountain, lies at 29,028 feet above **sea level**.
We climbed quickly to the summit.

Sun *noun*
The Sun is a star. Scientists think that it has a liquid center, surrounded by a large mass of very hot **gas**. In **orbit** around the Sun is a **solar system** of nine planets, including the **Earth,** the third planet from the Sun. Radiation from the Sun reaches Earth as heat and **sunlight**. This **solar energy** allows life to exist.
The Earth makes a complete orbit of the Sun once a year.

139

sunlight *noun*

Sunlight is the light that reaches the **Earth** from the **Sun**. All life on Earth depends upon sunlight. Plants need sunlight to make their food and grow. Animals feed on the plants, or on other animals. Sunlight is a form of **radiation.**

One side of the valley was in bright sunlight while the other side was in shadow.

supercontinent *noun*

A supercontinent describes one of the huge **continents** that may have existed very early in the history of the **Earth**. Some scientists think that the continents of today were once joined together in a single supercontinent, called **Pangaea**. (See illustration page 108.)

Scientists think that the supercontinents of the past were much larger than the continents of today.

surf *noun*

Surf is the foam and spray caused by **waves** as they break on the **seashore**, or on rocks. Animals and plants living in the surf are firmly fixed to the rocks, or live in burrows beneath the surface of the ground, so that they are not swept away.

The large waves made a great amount of surf as they broke upon the seashore.

surface *noun*

The surface is the outer layer of a substance, such as a **rock** or **mineral**. Many rocks have rough surfaces. **Crystals** have smooth surfaces. The surface of a broken **flint** is also very smooth.

The surface of the rock was covered in bumps and ridges.

survey *noun*

A survey is a careful investigation of an area or **region** for particular **features** or substances. A geological survey tries to discover the main **rock** types and **soils** of an area.

The survey revealed that the rocks contained many minerals.

swamp *noun*

A swamp is a kind of **wetland**. In a swamp, the water level is high and the plants growing in it are always surrounded by water.

The swamp contained an unusual variety of animals and plants.

mangrove swamp

swell *noun*

Swell is the movement of the open **sea**. The swell of the sea is caused by long, rolling **waves** that do not break at the surface. Swell causes boats and ships to sway and roll in the water.

As soon as the ferry left the harbor, we felt the swell of the sea.

syncline *noun*

A syncline is a kind of fold in **sedimentary** and **metamorphic** rocks. In a syncline, layers, or **strata**, of rock fold downward in a **basin**, with the younger rocks at the top. A syncline is the opposite of an **anticline**.

The geologist pointed out where the rocks dipped down in a syncline.

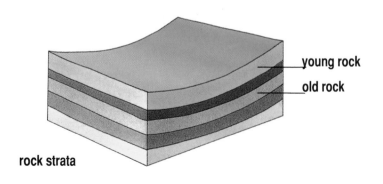

young rock
old rock
rock strata

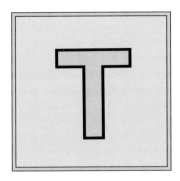

tableland   *noun*
A tableland is a **landscape** with a large area of flat, high land. The surface of the land is flat, like a table.
The outline of the tableland stood out in the distance.

taiga   *noun*
Taiga is the **forest** that lies just to the south of the **Arctic** region. The taiga contains coniferous (cone-bearing) and evergreen trees, such as spruce and pine. It stretches for many thousands of miles, mostly in Siberia.
The deer wander in the dark forests of the taiga.

talc   *noun*
Talc is a soft mineral. White to pale green in color, talc is found in **metamorphic** rocks, and contains **magnesium** and **silicon**. There are large **deposits** of talc in India and in Austria. When it is ground up, it is called talcum powder. The solid form of talc is also called **soapstone**.
Powered talc is an ingredient used in baby powder.

talus ► **scree**

tectonic plate ► page 142

temperate   *adjective*
Temperate describes a region or **climate** that is neither very hot nor very cold. The temperate zones lie between the **tropics** and the **polar** regions.
A temperate climate is warmer than a polar climate.

temperature   *noun*
Temperature is a measurement of how hot or cold something is. Temperature is measured in **degrees** using a **thermometer**.
The horses moved into the shade as the temperature rose.

terminal moraine ► **moraine**

terrain   *noun*
Terrain is the surface of an area of country. In a flat terrain, the surface is level, but in hilly terrain it is very bumpy.
We crossed rough, rocky terrain.

terrestrial   *adjective*
Terrestrial describes something that lives on the **land**. Most animals and plants are terrestrial, and feed and grow on dry land.
At the edge of the lake, the aquatic plants gave way to terrestrial plants.

Tertiary   *adjective*
Tertiary describes a subera in **geological time** from about 65 million to about 2 million years ago. (See chart page 64.)
The mountains of the Himalayas were formed during the Tertiary subera.

Tethys Sea   *noun*
The Tethys Sea is the name given to the sea that once lay between **Laurasia** and **Gondwanaland**. Scientists think the sea was formed about 250 million years ago when **Pangaea** split into two parts. (See illustration page 108.)
The map showed where scientists thought the Tethys Sea once lay.

tectonic plate *noun*

A tectonic plate is a section of the Earth's **crust** that moves as a single piece. There are seven major tectonic plates on the surface of the Earth and several smaller ones. Where two or more moving plates meet, the surface of the Earth may bend or crack and **earthquakes** or **volcanoes** may occur. One plate may move under another in a **subduction zone**. When oceanic plates

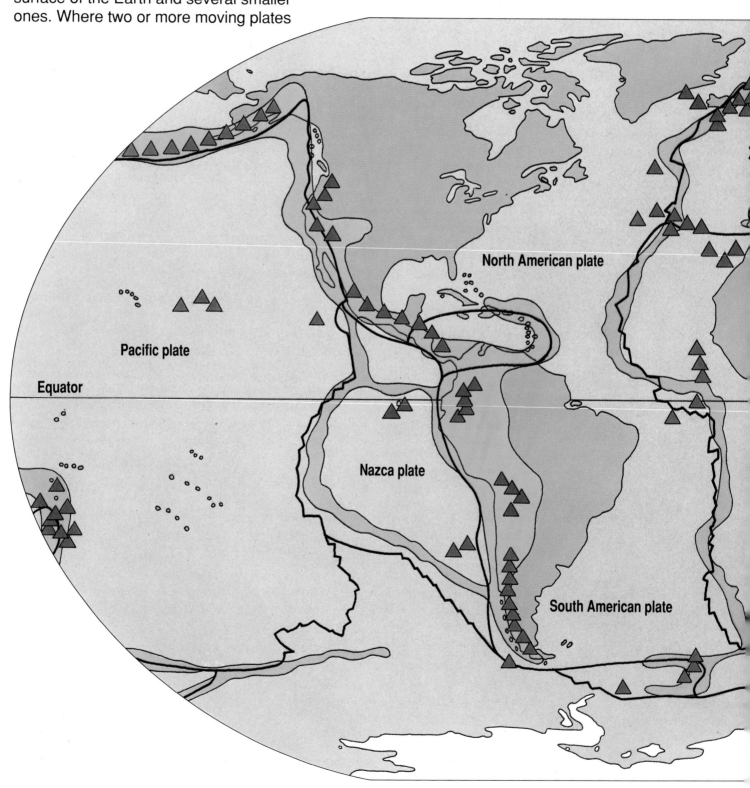

move apart, **seafloor spreading** occurs.
(See illustration page 34.)

map of distribution of volcanoes and earthquakes

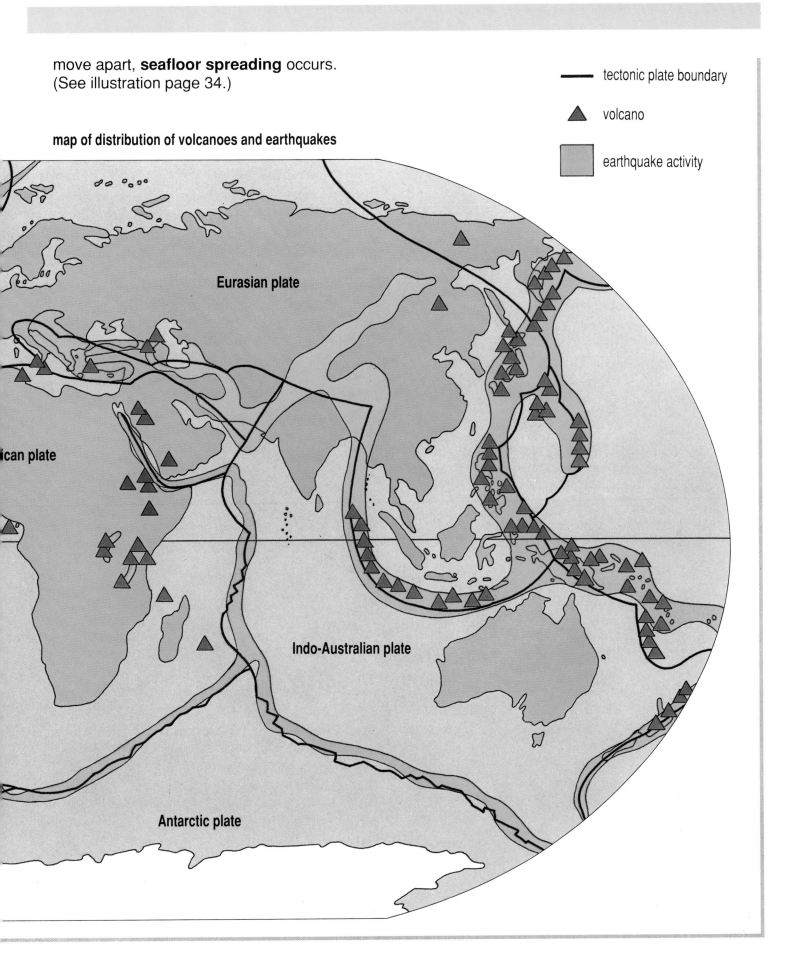

— tectonic plate boundary

▲ volcano

earthquake activity

Eurasian plate

ican plate

Indo-Australian plate

Antarctic plate

texture *noun*
Texture describes the size and shape of particles in **rock** or **soil**. It also describes the way the particles are arranged. Some rocks, such as quartzite, can have a fine, smooth texture. Others, like **granite**, are coarse.
The tiny rock particles gave the soil a rough texture.

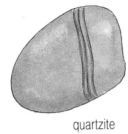

granite   quartzite

thaw *verb*
Thaw describes the melting of a substance that has been frozen. Snow or ice thaw when the **temperature** rises above freezing, or 0 degrees **Celsius**, 32 degrees **Fahrenheit**.
When the Sun came out, the ice thawed and turned into water.

theodolite *noun*
A theodolite is an instrument used in a **survey** to measure the angles between two points. It is a small telescope that is connected to a vertical and a horizontal **scale**. A theodolite is usually mounted on a tripod.
The surveyor used the theodolite to measure the angle between the hill and the river.

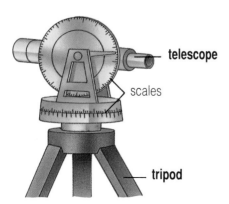

telescope
scales
tripod

thermal *noun*
A thermal is a rising column of warm **air**. Thermals form over hot ground when **convection currents** develop in the air. Many birds soar upward on thermals to help them gain height.
The glider circled slowly upward, using the thermals to rise in the air.

thermocline *noun*
The thermocline is found in the **sea** and in large **lakes**. The thermocline is the layer of **water** between the warm water at the surface and the cold, deeper water. The water at the top of the thermocline is warmer than the water at the bottom. The thermocline in the sea lies at a depth of about 325 to 650 feet. *The divers swam down to the cooler waters of the thermocline.*

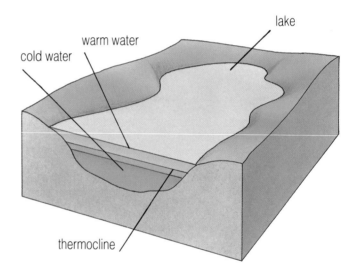

lake
warm water
cold water
thermocline

thermometer *noun*
A thermometer is an instrument for measuring **temperature**. Some thermometers have a column of liquid, such as **mercury**, in a tube. This liquid expands as it warms and moves up the tube. A **scale** on the tube indicates the temperature in **degrees**. Some thermometers have a digital display that shows the temperature in numbers.
Different thermometers are used to take air temperature and body temperature.

thunder   *noun*

Thunder is the sound made during a **thunderstorm** when electricity is released from **clouds**. Thunder usually makes a deep, rumbling noise. It is caused when **lightning** heats the air very quickly. We see lightning before we hear thunder because sound travels more slowly than light.
The sudden clap of thunder frightened the animals.

thunderstorm   *noun*

A thunderstorm is a **storm** that is accompanied by **thunder** and flashes of **lightning**. Thunderstorms happen when strong **convection currents** develop in the air. They can also occur when a **cold front** passes. Thunderstorms are common throughout the year in the **tropics**, but are almost unknown in **polar** regions.
The thunderstorm brought thunder, lightning, and heavy rain.

tidal   *adjective*

Tidal describes something that is affected by the **tide** or that is caused by the **ebb** and **flow** of the tides.
The tidal waters of the sea turned the river water salty.

tidal wave   *noun*

A tidal wave is a large **wave** usually caused by the movement of the **tides**. Tidal waves called **tsunamis** can also be caused by the **shock waves** that follow an **earthquake** or volcanic **eruption**. Tidal waves can cause a great deal of damage when they flood the land close to the coast.
They built a barrier to protect the farmland from tidal waves.

tide   ▶ page 146

tiger's eye   *noun*

Tiger's eye is a **mineral**, a bright, yellow-brown form of **quartz**. Tiger's eyes are used in jewelry as semiprecious stones.
Tiger's eye has a shimmering luster.

time zone   *noun*

A time zone is a region of the **Earth** where the time is the same. The Earth has 24 time zones. Each time zone is 15 degrees of **longitude** apart and is usually bounded by **meridians**. In each time zone, the time is a complete number of hours ahead of or behind the time at the **Greenwich meridian**.
Travelers have to reset their watches as they cross over into a new time zone.

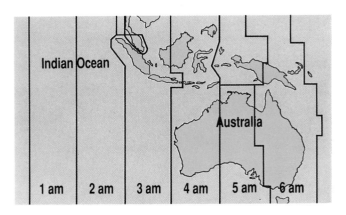

tin   *noun*

The **element** tin is a white **metal**. The most common tin **ore** is **cassiterite**. Tin may be used to coat other metals. Tin is used to produce cans for food and is also used to make **alloys**.
Malaysia is the world's greatest producer of tin.

titanium   *noun*

The **element** titanium is a white **metal** that is found mainly as a compound with **oxygen**. Titanium is used for making **alloys**, especially for building aircraft. Titanium **oxide** is used as a white color in paint.
The metal in the aircraft's wing was an alloy of titanium.

topaz   *noun*

Topaz is a **mineral** found mainly in **igneous** rocks. Topaz contains **aluminum** and **silica** and may have yellow, blue, or colorless **crystals**. Topaz is a semiprecious stone that is used in jewelry.
Many famous jewels have been made from topaz.

tide *noun*

A tide is the regular movement of **sea water** toward and away from the land. Tides are caused by the **gravities** of the Moon and Sun, which pull the sea away from the Earth. Tides with the smallest difference between high and low tides are called **neap tides**. Tides with the biggest difference between high and low tides are called **spring tides**. *The ship sailed away at high tide.*

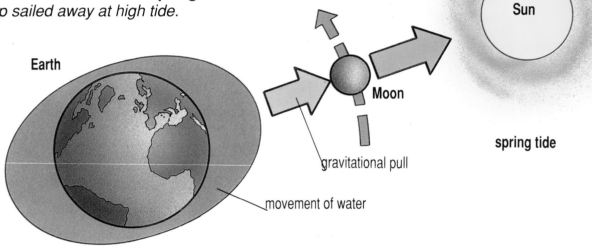

Earth

orbit

Moon

gravitational pull

movement of water

Sun

spring tide

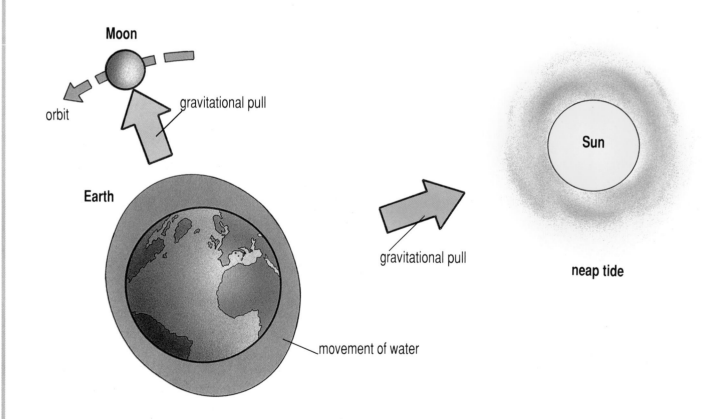

Moon

orbit

gravitational pull

Earth

gravitational pull

movement of water

Sun

neap tide

topographic map   *noun*
A topographic map shows all the **features** of a **landscape**. It includes natural features, such as hills, valleys, and rivers. It also includes objects that have been made, such as roads, bridges, and towns. The map uses **contour** lines and the heights of **summits** to show the **topography** of the landscape.
We used a topographic map to plan our walk over the hills.

topography   *noun*
Topography describes all the surface **features** of a **landscape**. These features include the hills and slopes of the land, the **soils** and vegetation, and man-made objects.
The topography of the area was dominated by rugged mountains.

topsoil   *noun*
Topsoil is the surface layer of the **ground**, usually made up of loose **soil**. The topsoil contains large amounts of **humus**. Plants are rooted in the topsoil and take their water and minerals from it.
The water from the flood removed most of the topsoil from the hillside.

tor   *noun*
A tor is a small area of **rock** that is exposed at the top of a rounded hill. Tors appear when the surrounding rocks have been worn away by **erosion**. Some tors at the top of hills have become landmarks.
The tor was outlined against the sky at the top of the hill.

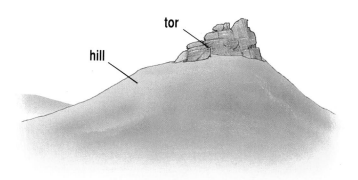
tor
hill

tornado   *noun*
A tornado is a kind of **wind**. In a tornado, the wind moves very quickly in a circular pattern around an area of very low **atmospheric pressure**. Tornadoes last only for about one or two hours, but they can be very destructive. They are common in the Great Plains region of North America. Other names for a tornado are a twister and a whirlwind
The tornado left a track of flattened corn across the field.

swirling winds

tourmaline   *noun*
Tourmaline is a **mineral**. The hard **crystals** of tourmaline are used as semiprecious stones. Tourmaline can have many colors, including black, blue, or red. Tourmaline contains **sodium**, **calcium**, **boron**, **silica**, and metals such as **aluminum**. It is found in **igneous** and **metamorphic** rocks.
She chose a ring with a dark red tourmaline.

trace element   *noun*
A trace element is an **element** that plants and animals need for healthy growth, such as **manganese**, **boron** and **cobalt**. Only small amounts of trace elements are required.
The rich soil had a good supply of all the trace elements the plant needed.

trade winds   *noun*
Trade winds are steady **winds** that blow from the east toward the **Equator**. In the **northern hemisphere**, the trade winds blow from the **Tropic of Cancer** to the Equator. In the **southern hemisphere**, they blow from the **Tropic of Capricorn** to the Equator. Trade winds are strongest over the sea.
The yacht picked up speed when it reached the trade winds.

tree   *noun*
A tree is a large, woody plant with a tall trunk. Some trees are evergreen and keep their leaves all year round. Others are deciduous and lose their leaves every year. The largest trees live for hundreds of years and may reach heights of over 300 feet.
Trees are an important natural resource.

tree line   *noun*
The tree line is the limit on a **mountain**, and toward the **poles**, beyond which trees cannot grow. Beyond the tree line it is too cold for trees to survive.
We walked to the tree line and then climbed to the summit of the mountain.

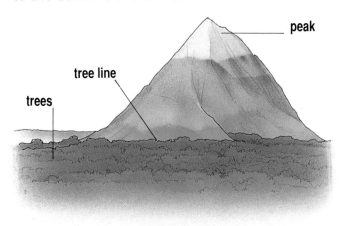

tremor   *noun*
A tremor is a **shock wave** that travels through the Earth's **crust**. The tremors caused by **earthquakes** can be felt over a long distance. Large, underground explosions may also cause tremors.
The scientists recorded the tremors from the earthquake.

trench   *noun*
A trench is a long, deep **valley** on the **ocean floor**. The deepest trench is the Mariana Trench in the western Pacific Ocean which reaches a depth of more than 36,000 feet. Trenches have steep sides and are often found by **subduction zones** at the edge of **tectonic plates**.
The seabed fell steeply into the trench.

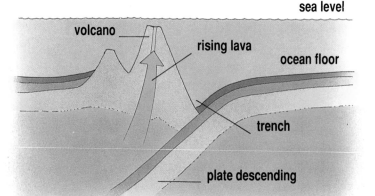

Triassic   *adjective*
Triassic describes a **period** in **geological time** from about 248 million years ago to about 213 million years ago. The Triassic Period is the earliest part of the **Mesozoic** Era. (See chart page 64.)
The first dinosaurs appeared during the Triassic Period.

tributary   *noun*
A tributary is a small **river** or **stream** that flows into a larger one. Most rivers are joined by many tributaries as they flow from their **source** down toward the sea.
We sailed down the tributary until it joined the main river.

trilobite   *noun*
A trilobite is a kind of **fossil**. Trilobites lived in the sea from the **Cambrian** Period until the **Permian** Period. The largest trilobites were about three feet long and the smallest about a half inch long.
The ancient rocks contained fossils of trilobites.

Tropic of Cancer   *noun*
The Tropic of Cancer is an imaginary line around the **Earth** to the north of the **Equator**. It lies at 23½ degrees **latitude** north. The Tropic of Cancer marks the northern limit of the **tropics**.
The Tropic of Cancer runs through the middle of the Sahara.

Tropic of Capricorn   *noun*
The Tropic of Capricorn is an imaginary line around the **Earth** to the south of the **Equator**. It lies at 23½ degrees **latitude** south. The Tropic of Capricorn marks the southern limit of the **tropics**.
The city of São Paulo in Brazil lies close to the Tropic of Capricorn.

tropical   *adjective*
Tropical describes something found in the **tropics**. A tropical **climate** is one with no cool season. It often has a heavy **rainfall** as well.
The monkeys lived in a tropical climate.

tropics   *noun*
The tropics is an area with a **tropical** climate. It lies between the **Tropic of Cancer** and the **Tropic of Capricorn**. In the tropics, the **temperatures** are high throughout the year.
Many birds migrate to the tropics in winter.

tropopause   *noun*
The tropopause is part of the Earth's **atmosphere**. It marks the upper limit of the **troposphere**. The tropopause lies about 11 miles above the **Equator**, but only about 3.5 miles above the **poles**. (See page 10.)
The diagram of the sky marked the position of the tropopause.

troposphere   *noun*
The troposphere is part of the Earth's **atmosphere**. It can rise to about 11 miles above the Earth's surface. The troposphere contains most of the water **vapor** and **clouds** in the air. (See illustration page 10.)
Most weather activity occurs in the troposphere.

trough   *noun*
A trough is a feature of **weather** systems. It describes an area of low **atmospheric pressure** that lies between two or more areas of high pressure.
The rain started to fall as the trough of low pressure arrived.

tsunami   *noun*
A tsunami is a huge ocean **wave**. Tsunamis are caused by movements of the sea floor during **earthquakes** and volcanic **eruptions**. They are particularly frequent around Japan and the Philippines.
Many buildings were damaged when the tsunami struck the coast.

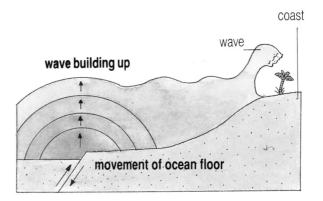

tundra   *noun*
The tundra is a flat, northern **plain** where no trees grow. The tundra is found between the **polar** region and the **taiga** in Europe, North America, and Asia. The plants growing in the tundra are mainly low shrubs, grasses, mosses, and lichens.
As the weather became warm, the birds flew north to breed on the tundra.

tungsten   *noun*
The **element** tungsten is a gray **metal** that is found as a **compound** with **oxygen**. Tungsten melts at higher **temperatures** than any other metal. It is used to make **alloys** and **abrasives**, and in some light bulbs. China is a leading producer of tungsten.
The steel alloy was strengthened with a small amount of tungsten.

turbulence *noun*
Turbulence is an uneven movement in water or air. It occurs when air or water flows rapidly past an object. The water in a **mountain stream** and the air in a **thunderstorm** are very turbulent.
The plane bounced in the air as it hit a pocket of turbulence.
turbulent *adjective*

turquoise *noun*
Turquoise is a light blue or blue-green **mineral** containing **copper**, **aluminum**, and **phosphorus**. It is a semiprecious stone that can be used as a **gem**.
Silver is often used with turquoise to make jewelry.

twister ► **tornado**

typhoon ► **hurricane**

ultramarine *noun*
Ultramarine is a bright blue substance that is obtained from **lapis lazuli**. It is used as a blue coloring substance.
Ultramarine gave the painting a vivid blue sky.

undertow *noun*
Undertow is the backward movement of water below the surface of the **sea**. When a **wave** breaks on the **seashore**, the undertow drags backward as the crest of the wave moves forward.
The swimmers were warned about the dangerous undertow.

uranium *noun*
Uranium is a **radioactive element** found in **pitchblende**. Uranium is the heaviest of all the elements found in nature and is used for making nuclear energy.
The uranium was transported in sealed drums to the nuclear power station.

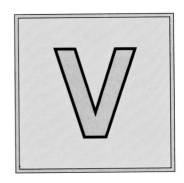

vacuum *noun*

A vacuum is a space that is empty of all **matter**. It is impossible to make a perfect vacuum. However, **air** can be pumped out of a container until it is nearly a vacuum. Outer space is almost a vacuum.

Heat cannot pass from one side of a vacuum to another.

valley *noun*

A valley is a trough-shaped dip in the **landscape**. Most valleys contain a **river**. A river creates its own valley as it slowly **erodes** the rocks and soil beneath. Valleys in high ground often have steep sides, but lowland valleys are wide and gently curved.

The river lay at the bottom of a wide valley.

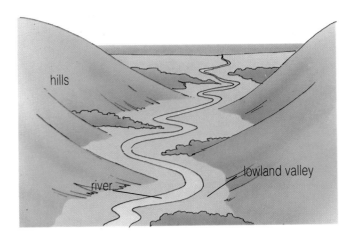

vapor *noun*

Vapor is the **gas** into which most liquids change when they are heated. **Water** turns into water vapor when it **evaporates** into the **air**.

After the storm, the air was full of water vapor.

varve *noun*

A varve is a banded layer of **silt** or **mud**. It is deposited each year in **lakes**, especially those near **ice sheets**. Each varve has one dark band and one light band. The dark band is deposited in the **winter** and the lighter one in the **summer**.

The scientist counted the varves in the mud to calculate its age.

vegetation *noun*

Vegetation is the total plant cover of an area or region. It includes tiny mosses, grasses, and herbs, as well as the tallest trees. As vegetation decomposes, it returns **minerals** and other **chemicals** to the soil to form **humus** and **peat**. **Tundra** and tropical **rain forest** are two types of vegetation.

The fire destroyed all the vegetation in its path.

vein *noun*

A vein is a **seam** of **minerals** running through a rock or stone. Veins are formed when liquids rich in minerals flow through gaps in rocks and become solid. The mineral in a vein often contains useful **ores** that can be mined.

The vein contained iron ore.

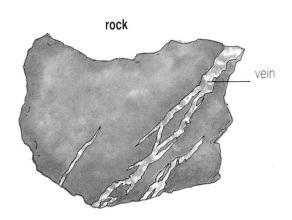

veld *noun*

Veld is a dry, open **grassland** found on the high **plateaux** of southern Africa. The veld contains mainly grasses, with few trees.

Herds of cattle grazed on the wide plains of the open veld.

volcano *noun*

A volcano is a hill or mountain that is formed from **molten** rocks. Active volcanoes send out smoke and steam and occasionally **erupt**. An erupting volcano gushes out ash, molten **lava**, and smoke. Volcanoes form either at the edges of **tectonic plates**, or at **hot spots** in the Earth's **crust**.
We could clearly see the smoke rising from the top of the volcano.

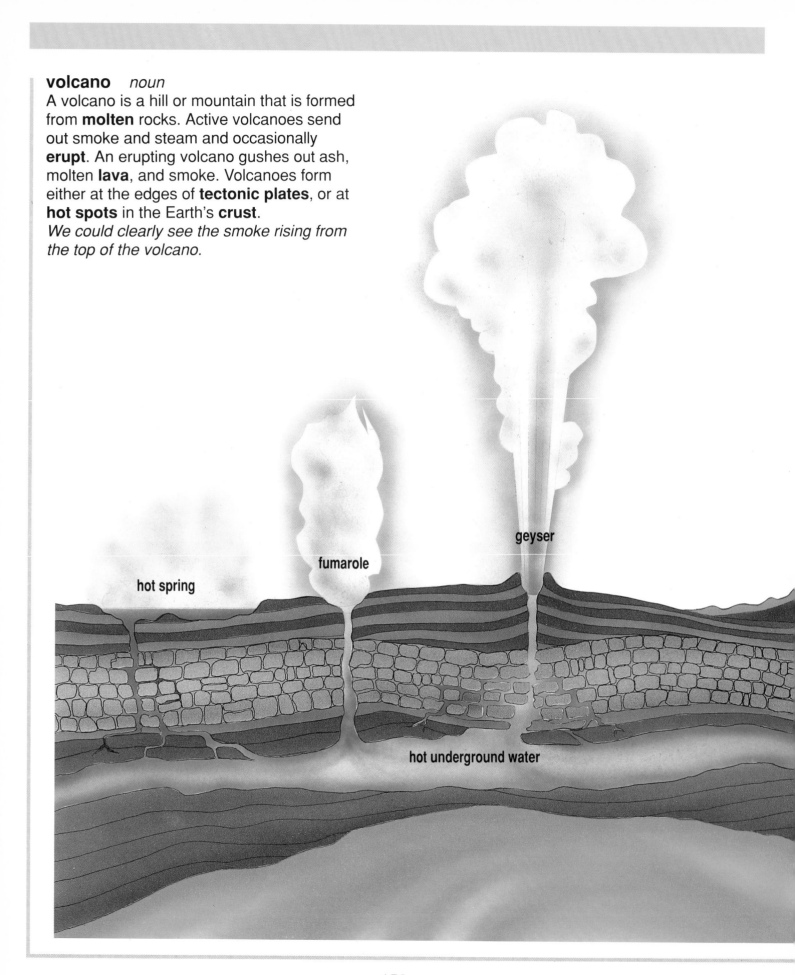

geyser

fumarole

hot spring

hot underground water

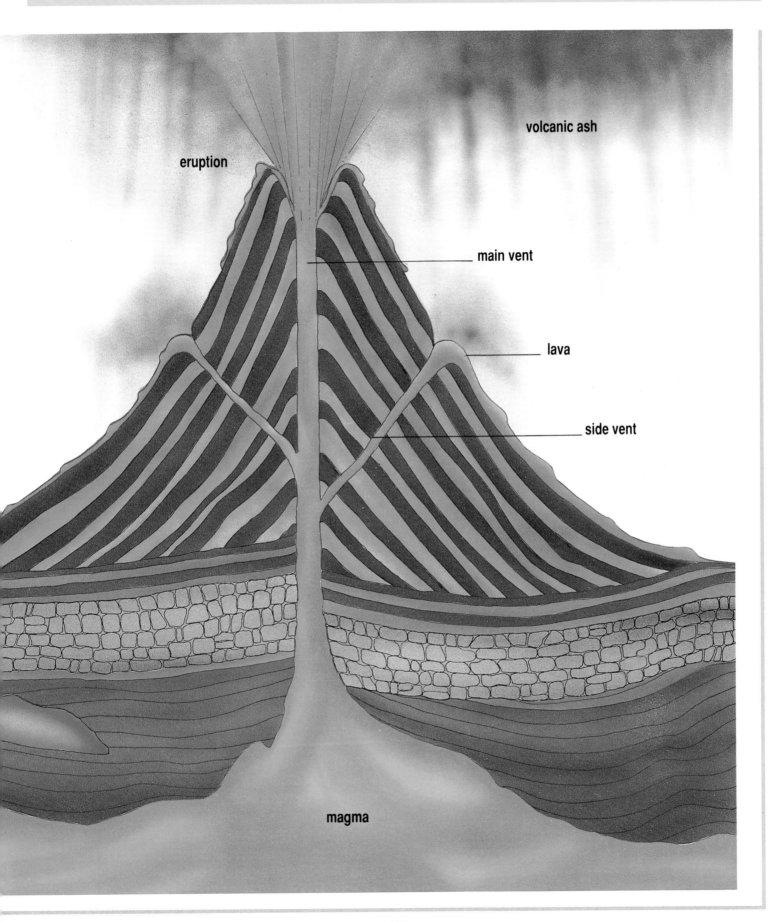

volcanic ash

eruption

main vent

lava

side vent

magma

vent   *noun*
A vent is an air hole or opening. Vents may be found in a **volcano**. When a volcano **erupts**, the **lava** comes out through a vent.
The lava gushed out of the vent and quickly covered the land nearby.

vermiculite   *noun*
Vermiculite is a **mineral** containing **magnesium**, **aluminum**, and **silicon**. When heated, vermiculite expands to become light and squashy. It is used for heat insulation and for packaging.
The precious vase was packed in vermiculite to prevent breakage during the journey.

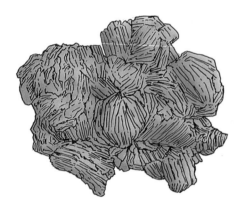

volcanic   *adjective*
Volcanic describes an area where the Earth's **crust** is active and where there are **volcanoes**. The Earth's crust is weak and there is molten rock, or **lava**, close to the surface. Volcanic areas may also have pools of boiling mud, or **geysers**, and hot water **springs**.
Iceland has many areas of volcanic activity.

volcanic ash   *noun*
Volcanic ash is the particles thrown into the air during the **eruption** of a **volcano**. Volcanic ash may rise to heights of about 10 to 20 miles in the **atmosphere**. The ash may travel a long distance in the air before it settles on the ground.
Volcanic ash drifted across much of the countryside.

volcano ▶ page 152

wadi   *noun*
A wadi is a dried-up river bed in the **desert**. In a wadi, the water only flows occasionally, or not at all. Wadis usually fill with water only after heavy **rain** or **flash floods**.
The camels walked slowly along the wadi.

desert

wadi

warm front   *noun*
A warm front is the place where a mass of warm air moves over a mass of cold air. A warm front occurs when a **depression** arrives and brings warmer air and lower **atmospheric pressure**. As the warm air rises above the colder air, many **clouds** form and often produce rain.
The temperature rose as the warm front passed.

water   *noun*
Water is a clear liquid with no smell or taste made up of **hydrogen** and **oxygen**. Water is mainly found in **seas**, **rivers**, **lakes**, and as **rain**. Many other **chemicals** dissolve in water. Solid water is called **ice**. When it is a **gas**, it is called water **vapor**.
Plants and animals can not survive without water.

water cycle   *noun*
The water cycle is the process by which **water** leaves the **Earth's** surface and returns to it. Sunshine and wind cause water to **evaporate** from the surface of the sea and lakes as water **vapor**. This vapor forms **clouds** in the sky, which drop **rain** to the ground or sea. The water cycle is completed when the water flows through the ground in **streams** and **rivers** and back to the sea.
Without the water cycle, plants and animals could not live on dry land.

water level   *noun*
Water level is the height of water in the **sea**, **rivers**, or **lakes**. The water level in a lake or **reservoir** varies with the amount of **rainfall**.
The water level in the reservoir fell during the drought.

water table   *noun*
The water table is the level to which **permeable** rocks are filled with **water** under the ground. **Wells** fill with water to the height of the water table. If the water table reaches the surface of the ground, water flows out of the ground as a **spring**.
Long periods of dry weather lowered the water table in the ground.

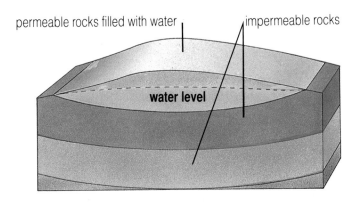

permeable rocks filled with water   impermeable rocks

water level

watercourse   *noun*
A watercourse is a **channel** through which water flows, or has flowed in the past. Sometimes, an artificial watercourse is dug to change the direction of a **river**.
A new watercourse was built to divert the river around the town.

waterfall   *noun*
A waterfall is a place in a **river** where the water drops steeply downward. A waterfall often develops where the river flows over a band of hard rock. The river **erodes** the softer rock below and the waterfall slowly becomes bigger.
After the rains, the waterfall became much more powerful.

watershed   *noun*
A watershed is the dividing line between two **drainage** systems. It occurs along the high ground between two **catchment areas**. The water on either side of the watershed flows into a different **river**.
From the ridge, we could see the rivers flowing from the watershed.

waterspout   *noun*
A waterspout is a spinning column of **water** rising from the surface of the **sea** or a **lake**. A waterspout is a kind of **tornado**. When a tornado forms above water, or moves over water, it sucks water into the swirling air to form a waterspout.
The waterspout rocked the small boats as it passed across the lake.

wave   *noun*
A wave describes the regular up-and-down movement of a substance. Waves are the ridges of water that move along on the surface of the **sea**. As a wave passes, the water rises and then falls again, until the next wave appears. Waves on the sea are caused by the wind and sometimes by the **tides**.
The high wind sent huge waves crashing against the coast.

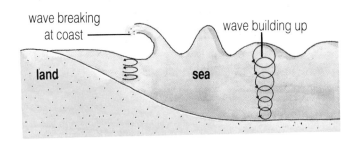

wave breaking at coast   wave building up
land   sea

155

weather   *noun*

Weather describes the condition of the **atmosphere** in a particular place. The weather can be cold, humid, wet, dry, or cloudy. Weather conditions such as these are caused by **clouds**, **precipitation**, **temperature**, **wind**, **humidity**, and **atmospheric pressure**. Different regions can have different patterns of weather. *The weather can change dramatically in just a few hours.*

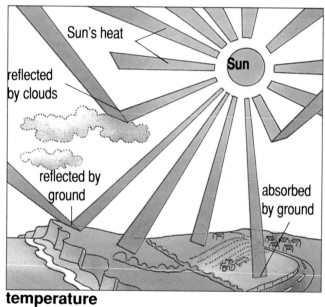

temperature

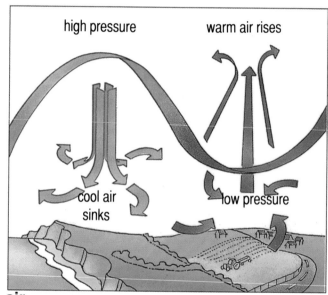

air

wind

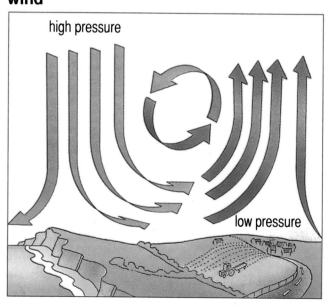

precipitation

weather ► page 156

weather forecast   *noun*
A weather forecast is a statement about the coming **weather**. Weather forecasts usually predict the weather over the next few days based upon measurements of **atmospheric pressure**, **temperature**, and **wind**. Satellites now measure changes in the weather from high above the Earth. These satellite measurements help to make weather forecasts more accurate over a longer period of time.
We went swimming that day because the weather forecast was good.

weathering   *noun*
Weathering is the gradual breaking down of **rocks** and **minerals** on the Earth's surface. Weathering turns rocks into **sand** and **soil**. The action of wind, water, ice, or **chemical** reactions can cause the process of weathering.
The cliff had been shaped by many thousands of years of weathering.

well   *noun*
A well is a deep hole dug in the ground. Wells are dug to reach a liquid or gas lying below the surface. Some wells provide water, while others are made to reach **deposits**, such as **crude oil** and **natural gas**.
A deep well was drilled through the Earth's crust in order to reach the oil.

westerlies   *noun*
The westerlies are a type of **wind** that blow from a westerly direction. They are found between **latitudes** of about 40 and 70 degrees north and south of the **Equator**. In the **northern hemisphere**, they blow mostly from the southwest. In the **southern hemisphere**, they blow from the northwest. Winds called the Roaring Forties are examples of westerlies in the southern hemisphere.
The westerlies brought a series of depressions toward the continent.

wetland   *noun*
A wetland is any area of **land** in which the surface is normally filled with **water**. Wetlands include **bogs**, **marshes**, and **swamps**. A wetland may contain fresh water or salt water, depending upon where it is.
The wetland covered the floor of the valley.

whirlpool   *noun*
A whirlpool is a circular **current** in a river or sea. It is caused by currents, **tides**, or **winds** moving in opposite directions. A whirlpool will drag floating objects down into its center.
Swimmers were warned of the whirlpool.

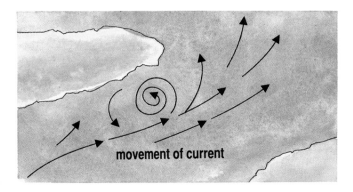
movement of current

whirlwind ► **tornado**

wilderness   *noun*
A wilderness is a **region** that is uninhabited and uncultivated. A wilderness may be a dry, sandy **desert** or an area of **snow** and **ice**, such as **Antarctica**. A **rain forest** may be a wilderness if it is unaltered by people.
Antarctica is one of the last areas of wilderness left on the Earth.

wind ► page 158

winter   *noun*
Winter is the coldest **season** of the year in a **temperate** climate. Winter is also the time when the days are shortest. In the **northern hemisphere**, winter lasts from about December to February. In the **southern hemisphere**, winter lasts from about June to August.
In winter, the snow covered the land and the rivers turned to ice.

wind *noun*

Wind is movement of the **air**. Wind moves air from an area of **high pressure** to one of **low pressure**. **Polar** winds are cold winds that blow down from the **Arctic** and **Antarctica**. **Trade winds** are **tropical** and blow toward the Equator. Many winds are regular and have local names, like the **mistral** and the **sirocco** in the Mediterranean regions. Wind force is measured on the **Beaufort Scale**.

The hot air balloon began to pick up speed as the wind increased.

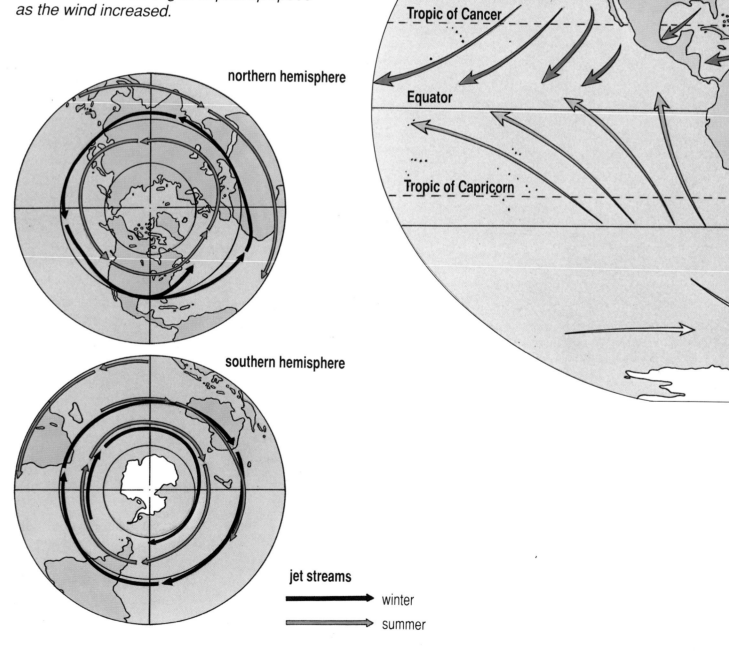

northern hemisphere

southern hemisphere

Tropic of Cancer

Equator

Tropic of Capricorn

jet streams

winter

summer

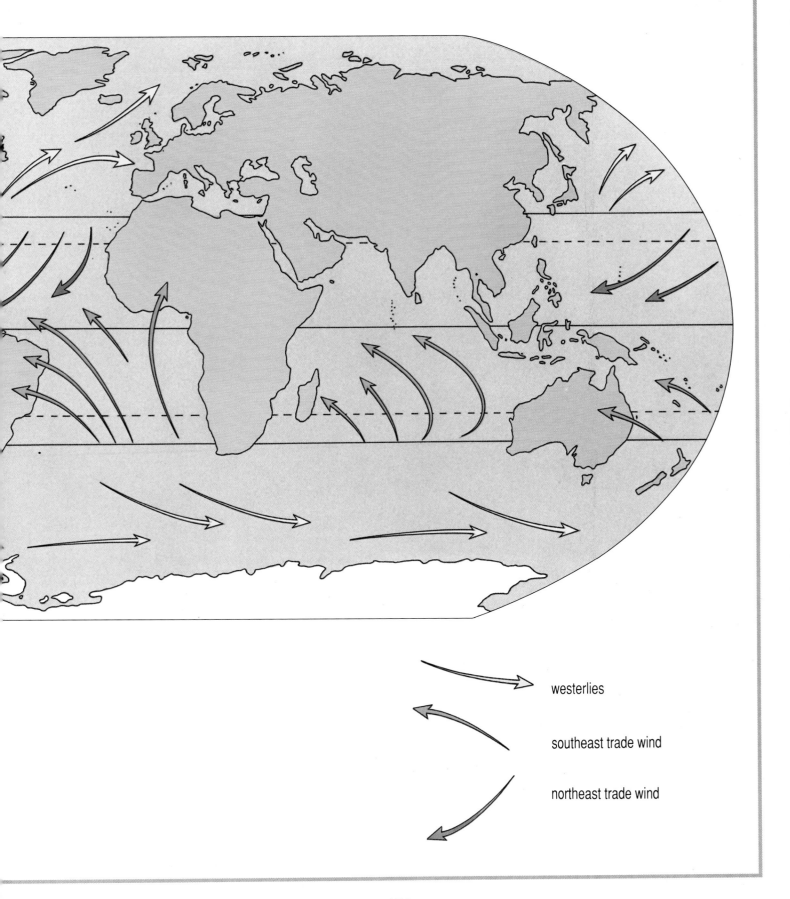

westerlies

southeast trade wind

northeast trade wind

wood *noun*

Wood is the substance of which tree trunks are made. Wood contains a **chemical** called cellulose that gives it strength. Wood is a valuable **natural resource** that is used for building and as a **fuel**. Wood is also used to make paper.

They planted pines in a large plantation to provide a supply of wood.

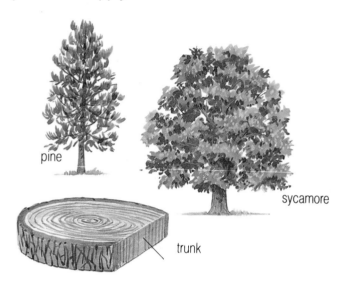

pine

sycamore

trunk

zenith *noun*

The zenith is an imaginary point in the sky that lies vertically overhead. It is also the highest point reached by a planet or the Sun above a point on the Earth's surface.

At midday, the Sun reached its zenith.

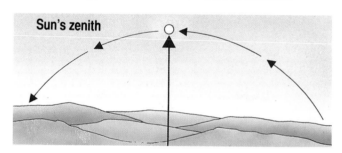

Sun's zenith

zinc *noun*

The **element** zinc is a bluish-white **metal**. Zinc is used to coat **iron** and steel. It is also used in medicines.

The metal coin contained zinc combined with copper.

zircon *noun*

Zircon is a **mineral** containing the **element** zirconium. Zircon is hard and heavy, and normally has a brown color. It is found as **crystals** in **igneous** and **metamorphic** rocks. Some forms of zircon are colorless and are used as semiprecious stones.

Grains of zircon dotted the sandy beach.

zone *noun*

A zone is a series of **layers** in **rocks**. Each zone may be distinguished by a particular collection of **fossils**.

The trilobites were all found in the same zone of rocks.